GWYN THOMAS

A FEW SELECTED EXITS

SEREN BOOKS

KU-580-306

SEREN BOOKS is the book imprint of
Poetry Wales Press Ltd
Andmar House, Tondu Road, Bridgend
Mid Glamorgan, CF31 4LJ

© The Estate of Gwyn Thomas, 1968, 1985

Reprinted 1993

British Library Cataloguing in Publication Data

Thomas, Gwyn, 1913-1981
A few selected exits.
1. Thomas, Gwyn, 1913-1981 — Biography
2. Authors, English — 20th century — Biography
I. Title
823'.914   PR6039. H59Z/

ISBN 0-907476-57-0
(previously published by Hutchinson & Co. Ltd.,
under ISBN 09-088350-0)

All rights reserved. No part of this publication may be reproduced,
stored in a retrieval system, or transmitted in any form or by any means,
electronic, mechanical, photocopying, recording or otherwise,
without prior permission of the author.

Cover photograph and design: Bryn Havord

Printed in Garamond by the Cromwell Press Ltd

Contents

I

And ten more dogmas bit the dust

The late summer of 1931 was bonanza time for me, if not for Europe. The results of my Higher Certificate examinations brought three awards my way. One from the Urban Authority was worth sixty pounds a year. A second from the County Authority would bring in eighty pounds. A third from the State brought the process to a peak with ninety pounds a year. They were going to spend more on me than on roads.

I became a notable figure. I had my name mentioned in a newspaper for the first time. My father was interviewed and congratulated on having given a new sheen to the poverty belt. Four neighbours tried to touch the hem of my coat as a healing tactic but were later found to be after my coat.

The University of Wales had, at that time, no department of Spanish, my principal subject. I had to look towards England. I applied to various colleges at Oxford for admission. I got two replies, both handwritten. One was utterly illegible. The more legible one accepted me.

Then the Urban and County Authorities, on the basis of a crude means test, cut my total take by £140. I was left with the prospect of storming the land's oldest university on so short a shoe-string my shoes even now keep falling off at the thought of it.

One early morning in mid-September my brothers and I sat on the steps that fronted our house to air the problem and discuss a solution. Not one of us said a word. We were stumped. The slump that had started in Wall Street had ground to a halt in our kitchen and showed no sign of budging. At that moment in time the dead could have been raised more easily than cash. We had heard of local lads who had made a fistful as burglars or as finger-men for some White Slave outfit, but we had none of the daring or suavity needed for enterprises of that sort.

We left the steps and made our way up the gully that flanked our house. With luck we would have enough breakfast to dent the frozen despair we were now wearing as a suit.

Halfway up the gully I heard a commotion from the street. I went back to watch. A small neighbour of ours called Nim Jones was belting down the pavement. Nim would have been about eleven at that time and had already made his mark on the life of the place. He was always running and communicating. However quietly, secretly, a thing might happen, Nim would get to know and he instantly became a vibrant wire stretched from one end of the village to the other, telling the facts.

I wondered what new secret Nim had wrested from the night. Nim was shouting my name and his face was blithe. This gave no clue to the nature of the news he bore. Rape, arson, theft, subsidence, all flowed with equal ease into the net of Nim's enjoyment. He stood at the gate, panting. Nim rarely came through gates or doors. He belonged in the free air.

'What is it, Nim? What's the fuss?'

'It's Mr Metcalfe.'

'What about him? Is he dead?' That was a natural question. Death had a great fluency in the district and we were surprised if it was not active somewhere or another. Our ears were always cocked for the burst of open-air singing from one or other of the streets around, which would announce a passing, and a straggling march of mourners to the Dark Meadow, our cemetery, a large patch of negation strung along two miles of hillside at the other end of the town.

'He's going to give it to you,' said Nim.

'Give what to me?'

'His trunk. His new, shiny leather trunk. For you to go away to the college.'

I was delighted but said nothing. Nim created and threw away myths as other people did fag-ends. Mr Metcalfe's trunk was a big thing in the street. We had been hearing about it for years but had never seen it. Mr Metcalfe had kept a small sweet shop at the bottom of the village. His speciality had been mint lumps, a type of huge humbug which, when it started moving from one clump of teeth to the next, cut down talking more effectively than a police raid.

In the days when my brother Walter had been studying in the back bedroom for his Higher Certificate examination he had been addicted to Mr Metcalfe's mint lumps. Their sugar gave him energy to survive the incredible hours he worked. The mint eased the indigestion that came to him after bending overlong over a too short table, and absorbing the smell of the oil-lamp by whose light I was later to work but whose wick I was never to trim as sedulously as Walt did.

During that period I was more devoted to Walt than any dog. He was the senior prefect in the school in one of whose lower forms I then was. Seeing Walt walk about the school wearing a green and yellow cap, especially designed for prefects, I had him tabbed as a Pharaoh at least.

The design had been made by the assistant Headmaster, a man deranged by inborn megalomania and a failure, through bronchitis and flat feet, to reach the front in the first world war. He hated the baseness and dowdiness of our town, and lusted to give us a large dose of hierarchy and ritual. Walt also wore a big prefect's badge in his lapel. That, too, had been designed by the assistant Headmaster. He had created a badge heavy enough to sort the men from the boys, and big enough to serve as half a breast-plate in the event of an emergency. The cap and badge were supposed to be worn in and out of school, especially in our part of the town, which needed a few Public School overtones, said the assistant Headmaster, as badly as it needed anti-rickets vitamins. Walt refused to wear the regalia.

He insisted on my walking to school with him each day. I had the biggest school-bag in the place. It had been made by my brother John, whose business was leather, and he must have put half his stock into that bag. I could have carried an extra pupil as well as my books.

When we left the house Walt wore a cloth cap of the kind worn by ninety-five per cent of the villagers. The other five per cent were a group of hedonists who wore bowlers to give their dandruff a feeling of space, and a clutch of professional mourners who kept their bowler hats perpetually on and joined every passing funeral, qualifying for a place at the meal of baked ham and pickles that followed with their headgear and air of controlled gloom.

Walt would never have dreamed of wearing anything on his head that would have aroused the attention and jeers of the younger among the cloth-capped brigade. Walt was a proud, refractory spirit. He was unlike the other boys in his age-group at school. Between the fifth and sixth forms he had spent a year out in the world doing a job whose nature I never discovered. It had aged him as drastically as the barnyard refuse used by moonshiners to hasten the maturity of their product. So, when we started for school, the cap and the odious badge were in my bag.

When we got to the bottom of the hill that led up to the school Walt would take off his cloth cap and put on the prefect's crown. Then on went the badge as I tucked the cloth cap all four feet down into the bottom of the bag. I recall that when I retrieved the cloth cap at the schoolday's end I had to shake the bag to get the cap within reach. The deputy Headmaster had spotted this manœuvre a dozen times. Walt knew. He had seen the assistant Head peering at us from behind a bush in his front garden with the crazed glare of Ben Gunn, the Treasure Island maroon.

He had an unbridled hatred of Walt, unusual even for a schoolmaster, a type often hysterical in his allergies. Walt's whole attitude struck him as mocking and subversive. He had opposed Walt's return to school. Once a boy had left school, he said, he should never be re-admitted. That might be feasible in gaols, but not in schools. Expose a schoolboy to the adult, non-academic world, and that boy was corrupted. Walt was the living proof, he claimed. He had seen us, as a family, cohabit with every group in the town hostile to gods and governments. He had even detected flecks of ungodliness in the way we played draughts in the Welfare Hall. The business of the cap and badge had just added an extra gloss to his emotion.

One morning he took his stand against one of the pillars of the school-gate. He watched me stuff the cloth cap into my bag and Walt pull the coloured cap contemptuously on to his head. He had the stare and stance of a man prepared for a showdown. Walt looked up at him, his face as grey as the flagstones we stood on. 'All right, then,' he said, and muttered to me between ominously clenched teeth that if the assistant Headmaster wanted to make an issue of it then he was prepared to slog it out right there in front of the school gates.

I grew at that moment. I was right inside a crisis of size and significance. There was a new pepper of potency falling on the previously tame surface of my puberty. Being admitted, in full view of battle, into Walt's confidence would hurtle me into manhood. The furtive self-experiments, the diligent duets of sensual curiosity with cronies in the Band of Hope would end, and my relationship with girls and even the women choristers who shared the stage with me in concerts, where I served as singer and reciter, and who tended to mother me, would go with a new ease and speed.

As I mounted the hill with Walt that morning I felt none of the misgivings which have since made me one of the most straightforward cowards of my time. The assistant Head hated me as much as he hated Walt. In his book I was already an

ambulant vat of ribaldry and anarchism. He had been told by
the local librarian that I could often be seen at the Welfare Hall
smoking and swapping lubricious tales with depraved groups of
older members, who often disturbed the concentration of readers
and players of chess and draughts with guffaws stained by sex
and tobacco.

He also took exception to my huge soft-leather bag. He said
it was a teacher's duty to keep a close eye on any young
exhibitionist who felt the need to come to school with what was
virtually a whole cow dangling from his shoulder. The cheap,
easily torn satchel used by those of my fellows who had no
brother in the leather trade gave him in some way a deeper
sense of security. The size and quality of my bag made me seem,
in his eyes, to be knocking on the doors of the County's ruling
groups, demanding parity or, on the other hand, I might have
the bag stuffed with home-made land-mines and disruptive
tracts. If a boy could use a bag to hide a prefect's cap and badge
he would put nothing beyond that boy.

The thing obsessed him, especially as I never allowed it to
leave my body outside the classroom. As far as I was concerned
it was one of the valley's diadems and I was looking after it.
Besides, it kept my back warm and waterproof. He would often
stop me on the school field and stare at the bag. He would mutter
that with a similar bag hanging down in front and a rabbit-skin
cap I would have been a dead ringer for Daniel Boone. At that
time I had not heard of the great frontiersman, and I could only
take it that he was telling the truth. He would say, 'What are
you gathering? What are you distributing?'

One afternoon I was walking around with a classmate who,
even on our levels of disgrace, was an outstanding pauper. His
name was Darnley. He, too, kept his satchel on and it was a
bijou object that flaked under the slightest strain. The assistant
Head stopped us. He pointed at my bag.

'Arrogance,' he said. 'That's all it is. Arrogance. There's no
need for a thing that size. Look at Darnley's bag. It's small,
modest, within his means and every bit as strong as yours. Give
me your bag, Darnley, and I'll show Thomas that he's as much

of a wretched show-off as that brother of his.'

He took Darnley's bag and subjected it to a violent test of strength. The bag came apart at every seam and landed up as four or five different parts in the deputy's hands. The deputy handed back the buckles to Darnley as if they were things he could confidently build on for the future. He also advised Darnley that if he were he, he'd sue me for the price of the bag and damage to pride.

Darnley did not sue. All he did was to ask me to let him have my bag after I had been thrown out of the school, which would surely happen if the deputy kept at me. He wanted the bag not to carry books but as a sleeping bag, because bedroom conditions in his home were rough.

Sex, I suppose, entered into this business quite a bit. There were many of my mates whose fingers had been starved of sensual delight. They had a way of following me around, impressed by the bag and the fact that my brother was a badge-bearing lictor. They touched the fine, yielding skin of the bag with cooing appreciation. Darnley went further and would rub his face into it.

The deputy noticed this. He was heard to say that he would not be surprised if I turned out to be the secretary of a group of sodomites being formed in the school's lower reaches, but planned to corrupt the whole school, using my excessively lush satchel as a lure. He even claimed that my work as singer and reciter was making me loose and lascivious. He had asked the secretary of the School Governors if there was some nineteenth-century minute which made it possible to have incipient lechers gelded. After I heard that I walked primly and cautiously past the deputy.

He had, he said, when taking the chair at concerts in the Welfare Hall and near enough to the stage to watch every twitch and wink of the performers like a hawk, seen me ogle the women performers between items. He conceded that it was only between items he had seen me do this. When I started to sing I sang at a volume that swept love right off the agenda. In that place of dedicated and zealous vocalists, getting and keep-

ing the true pitch was more important than side-issues like
bodily passions, even for a boy clutching with ardour the rud-
der of his central impulse.

Years later, in, of all places, Highgate, in a pub near the
cemetery where lies the body of Marx, whom the deputy de-
plored, he and I sipped at some drastically watered fruit juice
and checked on how well the scars of our shared past had healed.
The tissue was still tender, the pain sullen.

I tried to explain to him some reasons for his spiteful
attitude to the libido. The flat feet which had robbed him of the
military gait, the Don Juan strut. Life-long residence in a place
where repression had become an art-form, where too many
women saw life as a frigid riddle with no point in the middle,
who would have gone to their conventicles and tombs in a garb
of icicles if the icicles could have been bought in black. That was
why, I said, he had appeared to see lust in corners of life where
other men, sincere fanciers of lust, had never been able, even
with the help of dogs and radar, to find a trace of the thing.

He swallowed the last of his drink as if to say that the only
answer to this sort of nonsense was to wash it down with some
sober draught. The deputy (it is only now, reluctantly, through
the mists of strangeness and antipathy, that his name comes back
to me: Mr Denning) fell into a silence as sad as the aftertaste
of the fruit drink chosen by him as the cheapest line in juice on
view.

Then he said: 'How is your brother? How is Walter, the one
who was the prefect? Have the years changed him? Have the
years softened his spine a bit? Is he soft and flexible now, like
that monstrous bloody bag you used to lug about? That's a thing
I'll always remember. That bag. What did you hope to catch and
stow away in that bag? I had a dream. That one day the bag
would turn up at school apparently on its own, not hanging
from your body as it usually did, but with you inside, mooing
and frightening hell out of boys and staff alike. A good loud
voice, yours, and capable of doing that. Can't understand a sen-
sible, modest chap like your brother John fitting you out with
an article like that. And you, using that bag to conceal the em-

blems of authority, the cap, the badge, both my very own designs. That's the sort of thing that brings a curse on a man, take my word for it. When you mock at an institution that gives you your only true identity it is like slapping your mother. What institutions are you mocking now? Did you ever slap your mother? No? I'm glad of that. It shows there's a good side to you somewhere. Of course, you were small when your mother died, so you'd never have a chance to know what your feelings about her really were. Fine woman, your mother. Loyal to life, bringing up that brood and putting up with that undisciplined clown of a father of yours. As you get older you'll find yourself doing some odd things, things that make no sense at all. You'll be throwing echoes back at that buffoon. Watch that. Avoid echoes. Silence is the only sanity. Good singer, too, your mother. Fine, heavy lips that gave extra substance to every note. Heard her sing a solo at the memorial service to the victims of the 1920 disaster. Song called "Yonder, Yonder", the finest sung statement on the inevitability of heaven I ever heard. Gave a lot of solace to the bereaved. Even did something for my catarrh. A quiet weep is sound therapy. Don't despise it. Why don't you sing songs like "Yonder, Yonder"? The last time I heard you sing in public was with that little male voice group they formed in the Welfare Hall. A toothless lot. You had teeth, I'll admit that, but they'll go, don't fret. It was hard to follow the words of the songs they sang, being toothless and without discipline, but the few words that came through all seemed to be urging strikes and praising Russia. And nearly always off-key. That was deliberate, was it? Atonal? Well, I don't think much of that as a tactic, I can tell you. If life and love are not a sweet melody, as the song says, never let on that you know. If you can live in some kind of harmony with your chosen lies you are doing all right. You were only any good as a singer when you were sharing the stage with women. Bad weakness, that. Have you still got it? Funny thing, sex. Doesn't worry me now. Too old even to feel perverse about it. Thank God. Tell age to hurry up, Thomas. There's no peace or joy for the likes of you until the cold comes.'

I said nothing. His words had released waves of daft remem-
brance that washed the sense and sequence of my thoughts.

Then he said, 'You didn't tell me about Walter. How is
Walter?'

The question set racing once again the juices of that morn-
ing when Walter and I advanced up the hill to the gates where
Mr Denning awaited us. I stayed close to Walter. I wanted to
share any danger he might be in, ward off any blows that might
fall on him. I was excited by the sound of my great bag bump-
ing against my hastening legs. It had my cowboy fix pinching.
I slapped imaginary chaps and side-irons in the manner of
Colonel Tim McCoy, noted horseman, gunfighter and Indian-
killer of the early cinema.

There was no climax, no challenge. The Headmaster came
walking at his usual furious speed up the road that approached
the school, at right angles to the hill on which we were walking.
He engaged Mr Denning in some discussion on policy. They
vanished into the school.

During Walter's last year at the school I served him as a kind
of cut-rate djinn. I was there to serve. He studied right through
every evening and never left the house. I wanted to match Walt's
devotion to his books by my devotion to him. As I wanted one
day to inherit his rather smart suits, I wanted also to inherit his
slight stoop, his pallor, his peremptory, uncharacteristic way of
talking.

As long as he was at his table I remained at my post of duty,
which was exactly halfway up the stairs. I kept my eyes fixed on
the dim light from the oil-lamp which showed through the
small, curtained glass panes of the bedroom door. Any word of
command, any rustle of unease, and I was up the stairs like a
whippet, my hand on the bedroom door, throwing it open and
shouting, 'Want any oil, Walt? Any mint lumps from Mr
Metcalfe? Any fags, Walt?' And my joy was total if Walt
forked out a threepenny or sixpenny piece and sent me flying
down the street for any of these things.

I was most pleased when the order was for the mint lumps.
I thought the lumps did him the most good, and I could help

myself to them on the way back, which I could not do with the oil or the cigarettes. Often my loyalty and willingness got on Walter's nerves. He had a way, when excited by a line of verse or a probing aphorism, of reading them dramatically aloud. I always interpreted the sound as a summons and I was through the bedroom door and panting alongside Walter's table before he got to the last word of his quotation.

He said this cut down his studying time by one half and gave him, whenever he read French aloud in the years to come, a fear that it would bring me on like rain and fetch me shooting through the door. He also claimed that my quick servility forced him to buy so many mint lumps he did not need, he found himself at times swinging between a rabid itch and an edge of torpor.

I do not think those vigils on the stair did me much good either. The stairs were an awkward place to sit on and the discomfort and loneliness must have done something to chill my psyche. I might have been better off romping around the lanes and foothills with my fellows, probing the routes and testing the quality of the girl country. As it was, hooked to Walt, I might just as well have been a Trappist. My prurience simmered on no lower a flame than that of my companions, and if the local bardic festivals had offered prizes for sex-fantasy I think I would have had a ribbon or two to show.

But I noticed several of my contemporaries, at an astonishingly early point of adolescence, strut into an extrovert mastery of the love medium, squiring girls home from school, pomading their hair for long Saturday-evening sessions of close fleshly contact, canoodling boldly in the cinema and defying the stare of two ushers' torches which told them they were being observed and warned.

A boy of fifteen, after being bundled out of a cinema by two ushers, one a Calvinist, the other a wrestler, for unbearable daring in his approach to two girls, was named by us as the Creative Pupil of the Year most likely to be in jug when the rest of us were in college or the tomb. And, indeed, this same boy, at nineteen, fled the village with three affiliation writs fanning his rump and one demented father just missing him as he

B

boarded the train. He landed up in Slough, then becoming a complex of light industries meant to mop up the unemployed. We sent a round-robin letter to the refugee in a time of bleak emotional frustration, asking him for hints about the ways in which he had exploded to primeness.

He had become a lay-preacher, and told us, in his long reply, that he was now repenting his follies in a sustained, glacial calm. Something, possibly the sudden and breathless change of ambience and tap-water, had chilled his sensual gaiety. As soon as he had cleared things with the Labour Exchange and a friendly Probation Officer he had beaten himself black and blue with a brass-bound Bible and embraced a chastity which even Slough thought unduly severe.

*

But my errands for Walt would have been worth while if only for my talks with Mr Metcalfe. He was a rare man, an ideal social toy for the young in their troubled zone between ravelling dreams and half-formed fact. His lock-up shop was tiny and crammed with bottles. Some people maintained that he never left the shop, that he was immovably lodged there like a king bee in his sweet little hive. Anyway, he was there long before we went to school, and he was there to serve the men who came off the afternoon shift in late evening, long after we normally went to bed. On exceptional nights, when we were allowed to stay up late to celebrate some coronation, lunar eclipse, jubilee, or some simple bit of local confusion, the light still burned in Mr Metcalfe's shop, and until the last sweet tooth had withdrawn he kept up his bland traffic in mint lumps.

We were told that Mr Metcalfe had a fine head of hair. We never saw it in full. He always kept his hat on in the shop. Mr Metcalfe was a large man. Between him and the hat the sweets had a marginal look. He had bought a half-dozen of these hats in Seattle twenty years before and they were still going strong.

He had emigrated to America in early life and knew the cities of America's west coast as well as we knew the hills that flanked the village. He had moved all the way up and down from San Francisco through Los Angeles to Long Beach, Santa Ana, San Diego Rosario. He swept his hand along an imaginary map on the back wall of the shop as he told me of the enchantments of the Pacific and the Californian shore.

I was his best audience. I responded like a harp to the big vowels of his Odyssey. He had come home to look after an ailing mother. He was pledged to return as soon as recovery or death ended that particular problem. The mother died and Mr Metcalfe married a girl from the valley, a girl of striking beauty who had worked in London as a domestic help and had her portrait painted by Orpen. Mr Metcalfe had tried to persuade her to go back to California with him. She had refused and they settled in the village, Mr Metcalfe with his shop and his mint lumps manufactured in the kitchen, Mrs Metcalfe with thoughts of Orpen and memories of her picture in a huge room in one of London's academies.

She hated the taste and flavour of mint, and a distance developed between her and Mr Metcalfe, which would not have been greater if he had gone and resettled himself in San Diego. She had moved towards heavy drinking like a lemming to the sea. She became one of a group of loud, broad-bodied amateur harlots who drank stout by the bucket in one of the town's larger pubs, The Roseberry. Their room there became a clearing house for erotic jests of a rousing kind that had been known to have even old and dying men rallying to the flag. They specialised, too, in quick, back-lane adventures. Being free, skilled and ardent, they caused much bliss and at least four cases of pneumonia.

Once we saw Mrs Metcalfe brought up the road in a wheelbarrow, her face a cartoon of blind, lascivious drunkenness, her legs splayed to a point where her feet seemed, to my straining eye, to go touching the houses on either side of the street. My father was present, loud with concern. He was close to the action, advising the two men, who were wheeling the barrow, on the best speeds for pushing a loaded barrow up our type of hill.

He told us afterwards, in his most oracular voice, that Mrs Metcalfe's underclothing had been in a state of dramatic disarray. We asked him what he meant by that, but he said no more, hinting with his eyes that we would know all when we came head-on against sin's alloy.

The next day there would be a transformation scene as good as anything in pantomime. In the early evening Mrs Metcalfe would stride down the road to her meeting with the maenads at The Roseberry, her face splendid, her flowered, huge-brimmed hat grandiose, her bearing impeccable, a new Lily Langtry waiting for a new Prince Edward to fall besottedly in love with her. If we were sitting on the steps she would never fail to pause at the gate and smile at us, the only complete unit of graciousness in the valley. In her low, superbly modulated voice she would ask after our mother.

'She's dead, Mrs Metcalfe.'

'Of course, of course.' And the trouble would come tumbling back into her face and she would lengthen her stride as she made her way to her tryst with the nymphomaniacs in the town below. A few hours later she would return muttering, tottering and hostile. If we were still on the steps she would stare blankly at us and try to talk to us. The life had left her eyes, and the voice had lost its music. Sometimes she tried to push the gate open. When she did that we fled up the gully as if from the spell of a malignant elf. If she followed us up the gully my sister Nana would repel her, at first patiently, then with a frightening malevolence. Now and then Mrs Metcalfe would try to commit suicide, but half-heartedly and with instruments utterly blunt.

Mr Metcalfe threatened regularly to leave her. To make this intention plain he bought the trunk. He bought it in Cardiff, and when he and a friend carried it up from the station I was playing on the mountain and did not see it. But all who did said it was the glossiest, most glorious receptacle they had ever seen. On scores of occasions I heard Mr Metcalfe mention the trunk. Often when he was late in the shop, and he saw Mrs Metcalfe gibing at her own ghost on the way up from The Roseberry, he would stand in the shop's doorway and shout to her, 'There's an answer to this. I'll have that trunk of mine packed tomorrow. It'll come down this hill, packed and ticketed for San Diego, away from you for ever.'

Mostly she made no reply. Once I heard her say that as far as she was concerned he could stuff himself with mint lumps and go to the devil. She died of nephritis on my seventeenth birthday. Mr Metcalfe, some days before, had told me she wanted me to call in to be given her good wishes and a little gift. I called in. She was swollen, torpid, unaware. She had forgotten me and my birthday and the gift. For one instant her face brightened and that had nothing to do with me. She said, 'They'll be expecting me down there.' And she slipped back into the protective mist.

I felt hurt that she had forgotten about my birthday and the gift. Gift-making was a rarity in the village, and I argued bitterly against disease, transience and death for having left me in the cold. As I left the house I realised that I had twisted the dagger in my own wound. I had even forgotten to ask Mr Metcalfe to show me his trunk.

Mrs Metcalfe has rarely left my mind. The dichotomy of her being, the daily swing from a resplendent presence of loveliness to untouchable disgrace and exile jolted for all time my view of other people. In her quick transitions from radiance to dark she deformed my eye for ever. If anyone asks me to inspect and admire his agreed persona I never fail to feel that the agreed persona, submitted to my touch, has had its last chip and will now rush to collapse—and end. In the space where Mrs Metcalfe was, the light quivers, the air shakes and mocks. In the gallery of all my bemusements and terrors her signature is on virtually every article.

Mr Metcalfe, a month after his wife died, gave up his shop. On the last evening of its life he sent a messenger to the house and asked me to lay my books away for an hour and talk with him awhile. I blew out the oil-lamp, suspended the notes I was making on a book by Angel Ganivet, the remarkable Spanish diplomat and seer who reached intolerably gloomy conclusions about human experience and drowned himself, quite young, in the Vistula.

I made my way down to Mr Metcalfe. It was a calm December evening, but the street was full of noise. About a hundred children were at play, playing in their tightly defined territories. Their games were meant to set them screaming and drive older people mad. Doors were flung open and showers of abuse came shooting at the players from householders, many of them in their nightclothes, made distraught by the racket.

Football played with a tin by lads who never seemed to tire was a game that landed a dozen local neurotics in the Mental Clinic. Hop-scotch was played on the chalk-marked pavement, and many a hopper poised for a last vigorous hop into home-base was sent spinning by a boy or girl hurtling away in a game of hide and seek. This game, played by a mixed group, had sexual undertones, and on nights dark enough to encourage daring mischief there were voyeurs who secreted themselves in the more obvious hiding places to watch developments.

Twice I was forced off the pavement by chains of boys playing a game called 'Weak Horses, Strong Donkeys'. This was rather like leap-frog but played by two teams, one crouching head to buttock against a wall. They were leaped on by the opponents, and the side that got all their members on the backs of the crouchers won. This game played hell with the local necks and spines, especially if one had the spot right up against the wall and took the full force of the number one leaper, who was usually strong and heavy.

I often found my head against the wall, my companions being useful flatterers who persuaded me that I had the kind of breadth and squatness to make me a perfect anchor-man in this kind of operation. Frequently my head was rammed against the wall by the impact and as I was emerging from the twilight caused by that shock I was hustled back into the dark by the tenant of the house against which we had been playing, come out to belabour us for having brought part of the house's fabric pattering on his head.

One could never pass a group of boys caught up in this pastime without hearing groans and the rattle of slipping discs, for our bones were not of the best. Two boys I can think of who, in later life, as operatic choristers, became famous in choral scenes from Verdi's *Nabucco* and Rossini's *Moses* as captive Israelites. They had a long-rooted look of unanswerable misery that gave a note of heart-shattering truth to the ensemble. This they owed to years of that game played against every wall in the village that looked one bit reliable. Having their necks jolted and the wind knocked out of their bodies by vaulting playmates had opened out to them a world of oppression and grief. The game made a deep impression on me. Even now, when I bend down, I tense my neck and check carefully on whether somebody is running at me from behind.

As I walked down the road to Mr Metcalfe's, warding off bodies that came shooting out of the gloom, I stared at the great pattern of lighted lamp-posts that stretched far up the valley. Always it looked to me like a suddenly opened box of brilliants. That was one thing we chalked up in favour of the Urban District Council. Even when they were most bitterly under attack as a clutch of clowns, liars, peculators and forgers we always conceded that they had rigged us up with a fine set of lamp-posts. The lights were arranged in long parallel lines along the hillside, rising with the grace of a music manuscript from the wild cluster of lights in the townships that bubbled on the valley bed.

We had extreme affection for the lamplighters, all rather short and silent men. We appreciated their silence, for their task, to us, who would have dreaded unmitigated night in a place so full of disruptive angles and dislocated, unpredictable people as the valley, was solemn, hieratic, beautiful. For next to a baton to bring huge choirs baying into life, a fist of rhetoric to thrust a scalded congregation away from sin, a stick of chalk to bleach the ignorance of infant pupils, the lamplighter's long pole struck us as one of the lovelier instruments of living.

If anyone sees anything Freudian in this I don't mind. I see Freud himself as a bit of a lamp-post. And when sex fails and the imagination withers I shall seek out a place where they still have gas-lamps in the sloping streets and the odd, idle pole. My affection for the street lights of the valley has only one reservation. Watching their pattern come to fullness from the river's edge to the high horizon through a long dusk took my mind and eyes away from the stars that were trying to get into the act from above. Even now the night sky is as much of a mystery to me as the language of animals, the impulses of the wind.

Mr Metcalfe was alone in the shop when I got there. It was late in the week. Money was short and clients few. He offered me a handful of some sweet-meats called Rum and Butter toffees, which we considered high-toned and sensually rich. Mr Metcalfe told me to concentrate on the butter side of these confections, for in drink, he said, there was no assuagement. He had tried a spell of dipsomania, he added, at about the time when Mrs Metcalfe had started her long swim to the grave, but he had found the exercise pointless and he had called it off with relief.

He drew his hand down the imaginary map of America's West Coast and recited the names of the places he had known, loved, left and hungered for ever since: San Francisco, Los Angeles, Santa Ana, Rosario. . . . I recited the last names with him, the sound of the vowels seeming even more plangent through the Rum and Butter toffees.

'I'll go back there,' he said. 'Without those places I've been empty. Nothing has taken their place. And there's no forgiveness for a man who goes through life empty and does nothing to fill the gap. I'll go back there. I've got my trunk. Never used it. Why do you think I've hung on to it all these years? Must have been a reason. I'll pack it tonight. I'll be off in a week.'

But he never went. He tried to sell the shop. The valley's economic life at the time did not have a butterfly's breath in it. Mr Metcalfe decided to give the stock away. We filled two large wicker clothes baskets with sweets and processed through the village giving them away.

Nim Jones was a big figure in the parade and kept an eagle eye on the basket to see how supplies were going. Now and then he tugged Mr Metcalfe's sleeve and pointed out personal enemies among the supplicants, who, said Nim, would benefit from a denial of sugar.

'That bloke clips me every time he sees me. No loshin for him.'

'Loshin' was what our style of English made of 'lozenge'. We used it as a generic name for all confectionery. Coughdrops we knew as 'burny loshin'. But Mr Metcalfe put Nim in his place and said forgiveness went along with this tide of sweetness, and no one was to be refused or short-changed. We made a point of lingering in the darker, shabbier side-streets where the poverty seemed deeper-rooted than in other parts of the village, a sort of desperate penury that had origins independent of any particular epoch or social context.

From where we stood, which in terms of social relativity was about an inch from the ground, that huddle of five hundred or so houses encompassed as many and as sharply defined echelons of affluence, pride and debasement as London or New York.

In some of the tiny, hardly ever visited houses our pilgrimage with the baskets full of sweets came as a surprise and revelation. We met people who had been exiled from the streets by years of illness. These people existed in a state of vast, unbelievable resignation. They were prepared for anyone or anything to come through their front doors, bailiffs, elves, the Magi, a portion of slipping tip or crumbled mountain, the Angel of Death. But even they were confused by the appearance of a small army of boys led by Mr Metcalfe, carrying two washing baskets loaded with sweets and dishing the stuff out to a gay Utopian beat. We were told later that our visit had hastened a few deaths by shock, but that the victims had been so impressed by the charm and originality of the occasion they had died smiling.

*

'Here it is,' shouted Nim from the gate. 'Here's the trunk now, Gwyn. Your trunk now. That's what Mr Metcalfe said.'

Two men came out of Mr Metcalfe's house carrying the trunk. Mr Metcalfe followed them. He had his hat pulled down lower than usual, as if he wished to deepen the gravity of his expression. The trunk was magnificent. It was made of gleaming black leather, reinforced by struts of fine dark brown wood. I stood on the pavement to wait for Mr Metcalfe. He shook me by the hand.

'Won't need it now. I'll never go back now to those places. Santa Ana, Rosario. Your turn to travel now. You'll go to many places, I bet. You'll need this. Firm as a house and lovely as a rose. Never wear. In the night when the place was quiet and Mrs Metcalfe, God guide her, was lying still, I'd touch it and dream of being elsewhere, because it stood for the bit of me that wasn't snared in mint lumps and misery. Most of my heart is in it. It'll bring you luck. All the years you'll have it I'll be with you in a fashion.'

Nim was listening, greatly moved. He wanted to notch the occasion with his active presence. He asked Mr Metcalfe if he and I could carry the trunk up the steps and into the house.

'Of course,' said Mr Metcalfe.

Nim and I carried the trunk up the steps and set it down on the paving outside the kitchen door. My brothers came and stood adoringly in front of the trunk, stroked the leather and praised the craftsmanship. Nana, with her constant conviction that all things tend to end in a backlash of treachery or farce, looked at Mr Metcalfe warily. She had never regarded him as cordially as the rest of us. She had often hinted that, in ways too subtle for us to understand, it was he who had goaded Mrs Metcalfe into most of her excesses.

'You sure you won't need it? We could buy it from you. Or perhaps we could manage. There's an old trunk that belonged to our grandfather up in the shed. He brought it back from America. Perhaps John could do it up a bit. That's his trade. Could you do that, John? I don't like taking things from anybody. People regret giving. There's always a snag.'

John looked gloomy. He sensed that Nana's reservation had landed like a vinegar drop on the morning of Mr Metcalfe's gladness.

'That trunk up there,' he said, 'that must have been the first trunk ever made. Put two shirts in it and the bottom would be out of it. America must have been glad to get rid of it. No sincere animal could have played a part in the making of that trunk. It's mouldering away. I don't know why we keep such rubbish.'

'Perhaps it's only that trunk that's keeping the shed together,' said Nana.

'If two people carried that object loaded down to the station they'd get to the station grasping a handle apiece. No trunk. This is a beautiful thing, Mr Metcalfe. If I were an animal I'd part with my hide with pleasure if it could go to the making of so fine a thing.'

'You've got leather on the brain,' said Nana.

'I want Gwyn to have it,' said Mr Metcalfe. 'I'll never go to America now. If I went I wouldn't reach the sea. Gwyn has been a good customer to me over the years with the mint lumps and that, and often in the shop he's listened to me talking when it did me good to talk.'

'He listens too much to people. He even listens to that Nim there. Preachers, the agitators, gypsies, spiritualists, he listens to them all. One day somebody'll set him off on a strange tack.'

'You're hard, Nana,' said Mr Metcalfe. 'Your foot can get caught in a rut. I watch my step. That's all.'

Mr Metcalfe took out his wallet. He extracted a five-pound note and pulled it out to its full size. It was white, large and crinkled. I had never seen one before. Nim Jones stared at the note. He would not have been more fascinated if Mr Metcalfe had declared his independence under a new flag. The note moved me into a new dimension. The legend was that if you tendered one in a shop the merchant would insist that you sign it, with a J.P., a policeman and a clergyman as co-signatories to prove that you were neither a confidence man nor a forger.

'What's that for, Mr Metcalfe?'

He handed it to me. As soon as I touched it my being fell into layers of guilt and fear. I have always felt as uneasy with money as with speed and monoxide.

'Another little gift. I want you to spend that on an overcoat, a fine, thick overcoat to give you confidence, even a bit of a swagger. They'll try to make you feel a dwarf up there, in that place, and I want you to be ready for them, in a coat that'll be as thick as armour. And don't go to the Co-operative or any of the big shops down the town. Go to Mr Warlow. A meticulous craftsman, Mr Warlow. Old-fashioned, but meticulous.'

I nodded. Mr Warlow lived at the bottom of the street. He did not have a shop. He worked in the front room of his house. If one peered in through the window one saw some rolls of cloth and Mr Warlow stitching away in a gloom that should have made him blind years ago. He lived alone. I could not remember ever having seen anyone in the house but him. He was a large, silent man. He spent an hour or so each day standing on his doorstep, an inch-tape around his neck, not saying a word.

We valued him as a figure of mystery, and we were sure that people coming up from the town into the village would take Mr Warlow to be a kind of watch-dog, and walk more slowly. The materials he used were heavy and dear, his work painstaking. Every old person who died reduced Mr Warlow's trade. A silence from without was now forming against the silence he had projected from within himself. He seemed now to be wearing a double muffler of anguish. No one seemed to know the details of his private mutilations, but there was clearly something about cloth or the village that made Mr Warlow's seat on life uneasy.

Nim was overjoyed by the news. He raced down the road to warn Mr Warlow to prepare, for the day was at hand, to scan his bolts of cloth and pick out the heaviest and best, for an order was coming that would have Mr Warlow's scissors clicking as never before, and his hand edging towards the till.

I heard Nim shouting as he rushed down the hill towards Mr Warlow's. 'Gwyn's got a five-pound note. It's white and big. Five pounds all in one sheet of paper. It's going on a coat. Mr Warlow is going to make it.'

His voice was ringing and exultant, like that of a young

prophet proclaiming that equity and calm had come to settle for good among men.

*

The next day I received an invitation to have tea with the Headmaster. The Head was a short, reddish man of vast ability, frenetic impulses and a loud voice in the land. He was called E.T. Dictatorial, hating committees, he was roped in to bodies dealing with topics that ranged from the need for a type of Welsh chastity-belt in iron that would give a fillip to our gasping metal trade, to the cry for a more vigorous teaching of Welsh.

For my first three years in the school I am sure E.T. never foresaw the day when I would be a recognisable wheel in his department of European languages. I seemed fated to turn up before him wearing the tatters of some disgrace. Coming up to my fourteenth year, I was recruited into the amateur dramatic society to which my brother John belonged. The play was *The Rivals*, by Sheridan, and my part that of Fagg's Boy, a jovial minion. There was no costume for me in the hamper of hired garments. A local seamstress knocked up a likeness of an eighteenth-century teenage turn-out. The breeches were tight and there were a few lengths of lace arranged in such ways as would have foxed both Fagg and his Boy. From certain angles I could have passed for a decorated stallion in some bijou fête.

E.T. was delighted that I was taking part in this activity. Acting was bound to invest even a hobbledehoy like me with a bit more urbanity and poise. Even in a role as minute as that of Fagg's Boy, the costume and the context would cause something of Lord Chesterfield and Beau Brummel to rub off on me.

Despite his own early mouthing of Radical dogmas, he said, his brief meeting with the Cardiganshire earl, on whose estate he had worked as a lad, had taught him that the aristocracy were not dead to all goodness and that something might still be learned from them. When he said that he looked hard at me but he did not voice his reservations. He added that he was de-

lighted to have been invited by the dramatic company to take
the chair at the first night. I felt gloomily certain that with E.T.
lowering his brow at me, things would happen that Sheridan
would have wished to keep out of the text.

The first night was a buzz of confusion. Men would come to
stand at the door of the Church Hall and introduce themselves
as voluntary ticket-collectors. They would wait until somebody
handed them a ticket, which they would then hand over to an-
other voluntary ticket-collector and proceed smoothly to a seat.
In this way no ticket admitted fewer than ten people.

When the genuine ticket-holders turned up and found inter-
lopers in their seats there was a lot of action in the aisles, jost-
ling and even fighting between people who had paid for tickets
and people who had slid in on some high tide of guile. The
interlopers had a variety of tactics to delay challenge and
exposure. One of these was to use the fire-curtain, one of the
ugliest objects ever devised. It was a mosaic of no less than
eighty advertisements put there by local traders.

The space was small and the adverts barely legible, for the
merchants, even in a few square inches, had plenty to say and
often included along with the message a picture of themselves
smiling and looking enterprising and honest. For the semi-
literate and myopic, the curtain made the Rosetta Stone look like
a current headline. The audience tended to move forward to
have a closer look. Interpreters arose, stood on seats and handed
down the messages and identified the faces. Roars of denial and
abuse greeted the text of the advertisements, and derision
showered on the identified faces, for every trader in the town
had his little host of enemies, people who had been refused
credit or who had been offered goods staler than our basic
laments.

They worked up a fine head of steam. Shopkeepers were re-
ferred to as forgers, arsonists, adulterers, masters, if not the
inventors, of short change, short weight. An undertaker would
be mentioned and a special arrow shot through his name. 'All
right, go on, get a coffin from him. Your backside will be
through it in three weeks.' Or a grocer. 'He puts so much sand

in his sugar he's had to buy a private beach.' Or an ironmonger. 'He's the one in the line of trade that sells paraffin that *puts* out the match.'

Often someone would pluck the trouser leg of the interpreters and demagogues and tell them to get out of the seats that had been paid for by someone else. These plaintiffs would then be accused of being the very merchants who were being assailed and they quickly fled.

It could be a shocking scene. I saw E.T. rise in wrath from his presidential chair and roar a demand that the whole outrageous hallful be crated and exported to Botany Bay. He caught sight of me and his eyes were heavy with the suspicion that I had played some seminal part in the trouble, having possibly briefed the voluntary ticket-collectors, lashed the mob as a whole into a white heat of rage against the cash-nexus advertised on the fire-curtain, and distributed enough lynching rope to have the entire Chamber of Trade dangling before the night was out.

I was having an anxious time of it. Between E.T.'s eyes, which seemed to follow me around as I moved about the hall, checking on the temperature of tumult and advising the quarrellers to calm down in preparation for the idiom of Sheridan, which would be difficult for an ear accustomed to the sort of *ad hoc* English which we had thrown up out of fragments of Welsh, the dialects of a dozen or so English provinces lashed together by what socially was the equivalent of the compelling haste of war. The older North Welsh immigrants, unexposed as yet to any formal education in the new language, tended to speak English backwards, and the others had not yet settled down to decide in what direction their speech was supposed to be going.

On top of this, my brother John and the actor playing Fagg were worried about me. They kept appearing suddenly before me and asking, in voices made sharp by tension, if I knew my part. It was a small part. I knew all six words of it, but they were hard to persuade. I had put my costume on early in the evening. I had got fed up with the fuss and clamour of the men's changing-room. (Most of our actors were men of great talent and hot imagination, whose lives were lived on levels sensationally below the level of even their tiniest dreams. Put them in the costume of another more elaborate age and you could hear the jaws of their Bovaric Angle go roaring back.)

I would have been wiser to stay in the dressing-room instead of mingling with the public. Most of them had no idea of the period in which the play was set, and, seeing me in the lace and breeches belonging to Fagg's Boy, thought I might be no more than an oddly dressed civilian customer. The zone at the time was full of people who could afford few new garments. They would disinter, from under the dust and junk of attics, clothes that had belonged to grandfathers and grandmothers, and a turnout of extrovert paupers in one of the poorer streets had the air of an untidy pageant.

I had kept on my County School cap to remind E.T. and others that I was not on indefinite leave from 1927. The lace and breeches, the first hanging in functionless disarray, the second of a pinkish colour and skin-tight, struck the half-naked look of modish underwear.

I attracted the attention of a sexual eccentric, a small, gaunt man whose failing hair he kept thinning by running his unhappy hands through it. He was said to express himself in the oddest ways in categories that no one wanted to discuss. But the eccentric's movements were swift and stealthy, and although he was watched with care and curiosity nobody could ever track down the exact shadow in which he was being shady. Youths whom he frequented, when questioned, would look astonished and say nothing.

He seemed to be keeping my breeches under constant survey. I do not know what effect those breeches had on him, but it was powerful. His eyes blinked and his mouth drooped. I had a feeling that at some point of the evening I might have to call on Fagg to help his Boy.

By the time E.T. got up from his chairman's place to introduce the play I was in a high state of anxious excitement. I was still in the auditorium, puzzling people, in the dress of Rousseau and talking about the idiom of Sheridan. Some of my listeners thought that I was referring to a man called Sheridan who, a few years before, had stood as the Conservative Parliamentary candidate in the town. He had spoken in a very cut-glass way and lost his deposit. His views were as hairy as old apes and, given his head, he would have had gunboats patrolling the local river, quelling all natives whose loyalty to king and country wavered in any respect. I got a clip or two from people who thought I was doing an initial canvas for the defeated candidate, and proclaiming by my costume that the thinking of Sheridan the Tory was as laggard as ever.

I got a message telling me to stop fooling about in the public arena and report to the wings where the producer had a final word for me. I was on my way when I heard E.T. mention my name. He was glad, he said, to have a pupil of his playing an important part in an enterprise of this kind. Many a botched life, he hinted, had been redeemed by public service of this type. He mounted his favourite horse, Overseas Service. He would not be surprised, he said, to see me, after gaining address and confidence in this experience, ripen towards colonial or missionary work in Africa. He said it in the firmest tones of prophecy.

I could feel myself doing an instant switch from *The Rivals* to the Limpopo. I had an urge to go and tell him that my part was neither large nor important, being certain that when he heard it, all six stammered words, he would think that I, off my own bat and to incommode the producer, had sheared my bit of Sheridan down to the bare bone.

All these worries brought on a strong wish to urinate. There was only one water-closet in the hall and that had been made over to the ladies. The vicar who designed the place had felt that with one toilet and a stage he had conceded enough to pleasure. I was told brusquely by the actor playing Fagg to go and relieve myself against the hall's back wall. Some diocesan sub-committee had granted this dispensation.

The rear of the hall was very dark and every shadow had its special wind. The lady who had made my breeches had, through

C

haste or ignorance, failed to provide them with any kind of cod-
piece. I had to pull them down. The night air chilled me to the
bone, denying me fluency. I slumped, as still as a statue by
Benjamin Haydon, against the wall. I became aware of holes in
the darkness a few yards away. It was the sexual eccentric and
he was eyeing me as if he had struck gold. He moved rapidly
towards me. I bolted, my breeches at half-mast. I went spinning,
but got up in time to avoid the clutches of the pederast or what-
ever branch of the service he was in. He also went spinning,
possibly through passion, for a boy with satin around his loins
was a rare sight in that place. More likely it was the pantherish
pace at which he came in for the kill combined with the extreme
roughness of the ground surface around the hall.

I got back into the wings and awaited my entrance. I missed
my cue-line and was pushed on to the stage. It was done too
roughly. I collided into Fagg with a force that had us both
tottering. There was a lot of laughter, which seemed to say that
while most of the audience had been pretty cool towards Sheri-
dan's dialogue, the broader effects, the belly-laughs, were in four
safe hands. But there was something more. I noticed a lot of
people not only laughing but pointing at their heads. I had come
on stage still wearing my County School cap. E.T. stood up and
gave the customers a look which said : And that's what you're
paying rates for.

Rain was another thing that made our relationship slow to
knit. I lived a good distance from the school, down one long
hill, then another, a gloomy highway called Cemetery Road. At
the bottom of Cemetery Road was the corpse of a flooded col-
liery. We were told that if one lay down on the pavement, one's
ear pressed tightly to the stone, the other ear plugged to keep
out surface noises, one could hear from far below the glugging
of the waters that had destroyed the pit.

One of the masters who passed that way once reported me to
E.T. for a whole week's peculiar conduct. On the morning of
Monday, Tuesday and Wednesday he had caught me smoking
in a back lane, showing off before some companions, inhaling
with a bravura and depth that browned my knee-caps. On

Thursday morning, being out of fags, I thought I would brighten the sad, long walk by listening to the spectral waters still lapping around their victims down below.

I was spotted by the master, lying full length on my side, my head resting on my great leather bag. I had tried placing my ear squarely on the stone of the sidewalk, but the touch of it had aggravated a long-standing mastoid trouble. So I had the bag between me and the flagstones. I got what I took to be my best spotting of the subterranean wash, but it was probably the rustle of the leather.

The master reported that seeing me in this position after catching me three times puffing at fags in the back lane, he had concluded that I was either asleep, maddened by smoke or waiting for the opium man.

The place was plagued by floods. Rain was intense and the valley narrow. After a few days of hard rain a thousand rivulets came rushing down the hillsides, white with rage. The frequency of rain, and when it came it came in deadly earnest, caused us to be misled about the amount of virtue in the town. Whenever people saw a funeral making its way to the graveyard in the teeth of the monsoon they would say, without checking on who the deceased was, 'Blessed is the body that the rain falls on.' We saw many a proven villain do the last walk with a tail of drenched mourners.

Some of the floods were severe and made boating a part of the curriculum in whole stretches of the town. The boats were looted from a recreation lake in one of the valley towns meant, with rowing and boating facilities, to be a Lido. The water had leaked away through a huge fissure caused by subsidence. They failed to sell the boats but had an offer for the fissure from a mining prospector who thought he saw something dark enough to be coal at the bottom of the gash.

There was always a fine body of volunteers to man the boats in a flood emergency. They must have been mariners *manqués* because they had the little fleet assembled while the first puddles were in formation. Each boat had two sets of oars and four sets of woodworm and sank at the instant of launching. One of our tourist attractions was the bobbing waterproof hats of the rowers as they tried to rescue the rations from their vanished craft. People marooned in their homes would often hide, fearful of drowning the hard way, until the oarsmen, hallooing for survivors, had passed.

But the floods which interested us were the smaller affairs: brooks made unfordable, back lanes turned into rivulets, any casual stretch of moving water which could figure as a legitimate hindrance on our journey down one side of the valley and up the other on our way to school. Dressed up in gaiters, our ears stretched for the sound of any new, large freshet, we looked like small, episcopal divines.

E.T. never accepted the story of these localised floods. He lived well away from the river and was nowhere as closely in touch with water as we were. He conceded that the hills were soaked after centuries of cloud-bursts, but he accused us of kicking the hillside in selected places to provoke a stream that would deluge some voter's kitchen and provide us with an excuse for turning up to school so many weeks late we were threatening to put the whole terminal system in jeopardy.

He blamed much of this on the gaiters we wore. Five or six boys from my section of the town had bought them and tended to wear them, rain or shine, feeling exposed without them. They came very high up the leg and made our gait unnatural. Each gaiter was tied by about a furlong of boot-lace passed through a record number of lace-holes, and to get them lashed to the leg in time for school meant you had to get up as early as the milkman. My companions and I, between having the gaiters abrading the fork and moving slowly in the face of heavy rain, had the movement of spacemen or cautious bishops, and the look of those Hessian mercenaries who fought against Washington.

E.T. claimed that the gaiters had made our thinking tortuous and false. He saw us as shuffling about like a little platoon of Jesuits, encountering floods where other people saw everything as dry as a bone. He came to check on us one morning. He found us sitting on the river bank, looking at the swiftly falling river. He was accompanied by Mr Denning, who loved patrolling the town during school hours, spotting and fixing delinquents. The rain had gone on for a week and we had a good run of delays and absences from school. We had walked about looking as anxious as Noah and petitioning for more water and fresh nails and wood.

We watched E.T.'s face and Mr Denning's with comfortless interest. For a minute or so E.T. said nothing. Mr Denning was muttering something, and one of the sharper-eared lads said that Mr Denning was deploring the fact that in the course of our adventures we had not discovered a lagoon into which we might have fallen and failed to be fished out of.

Then E.T. said, 'A pack of hydrophiles, that's what they are. Swimming out of the social contract. But Rousseau never saw this kind of approach. It's those gaiters, I'm sure.'

Mr Denning's comment was soft but quite audible. 'A set of bloody hydrophiles, that's what they are.' Mr Denning always had a mania for broadening the script a bit. He shepherded us back to the school and drove us up the hill like a sheriff bringing in the James Brothers.

E.T. forbade us to follow the devious paths through the back lanes of the places where practised dowsers of our type would never find it hard to discover some patch of water that would strike us as impassable. He gave us orders to take only the road that came swiftly and shortly through the town.

After that we had to exploit the simple rain. If we came across a defective chute from which the rain came pouring down we stood beneath it until soaked. We were well supplied. The town did not seem to contain one roof that did the right thing with water. Versailles could have done no better for cascades. We shed our gaiters to make quite certain that we got to the school too wet for instruction. There was an unspoken rule that if a boy from the further reaches of the rain-ridden valley reached school so wet that he would cause a pool to form in the classroom or would surely catch pneumonia if subjected to the cold air and draughts of the building, a building meant to punish, not assuage, the boy should be allowed to sit in the cellar, near the big boiler.

The cellar became as popular as the Riviera. It would have been all right if it had been used only by the genuinely drenched, the hard core of veterans like myself who lived in an area of known flooding, lads who, in the hottest stretches of June, never seemed able to arrive at the school dry. We found the cellar being shared by interlopers of all kinds, boys who travelled down the valley in tram-cars, on subsidised tickets, boys with long and splendid macs that kept the rain off. We sat on the piles of coke that surrounded the stove waiting for our clothes to steam back to normal, and smoking like chimneys as we emptied our packets of cheap cigarettes.

Between the steam, the cigarette smoke and the smoke that rose from the stove, which seemed for ever clogged, the air of the cellar was impenetrable. The windows of the cellar admitted no light at all, and I never saw any sort of gas or electricity lighting. It was a striking sight. Thinking of it I am always reminded of the Court of Beggars in operettas about François Villon, where blind beggars shed their eye-shades, cripples their crutches and all together sang songs that threatened the Duke of Burgundy. We did not sing, except very softly, so as not to invite interference.

No one would have known we were there but for the glow of our fags and the sound of our voices as we lapped up jokes and tobacco. Our clothes tended to blend with the coke. If anyone came down the cellar steps we dapped our cigarettes and froze into postures of sadness to suggest that we wanted nothing more fervently than to join the unsoaked in the main building above, enjoying the happy traffic in literacy.

Our conversation, credibly in an ambience so like that of a tiny war, was stridently obscene. There were few minds there that would not have yielded a set of cross-sections fit for Christmas dispatch to the Lord Chamberlain and his shearers.

It was this that got us into trouble with the caretaker, and led to the break-up of the cellar-set. The caretaker was a man who could have stepped with ease into any mythology. He was called Mr Williams the Quarry, a title which foxed many of the boys.

I knew its source. I lived near the disused quarry where Mr Williams had once lived in a cottage before becoming the resident caretaker of the County School. He was also a deacon of the chapel of which I was a member. These facts, in relation to Mr Williams, gave me a sense of shared power.

He had been a miner for a long time before moving up into this comparatively smooth, new employment. As a miner he had been so prone to accidents he had won a lot of sympathy. If a stretch of roof lapsed it seemed to insist on having Mr Williams beneath to make the landing less brusque and brutal. He broke each of his limbs repeatedly. One of his regular companions at the coal-face was a man who was trying to distinguish himself in the first-aid section of the St John Ambulance Brigade, and a clumsier hand with a splint could not have been found. He was the man who always managed to give rough, primary treatment to Mr Williams after each fresh fracture.

Mr Williams had more mis-set bones than any other man walking. When a new accident happened he would demand that a first-aid man of greater tact and experience be found, but the same man, working largely in the dark and from a textbook that had been mutilated by men needing paper to light their pipes, would turn up and work another significant bit of mischief on Mr Williams' bones.

His legs were most atrociously bowed, but this overt badge of misfortune did him no lasting harm. When he foreswore levity and worked his way gravely into the diaconate of our chapel his sails were set for preferment. The combination of woe and piety and a serious interest in social reform put him in strong with the local Council, and he walked away with the caretakership when the incumbent perished of the Spanish influenza in 1919.

By most of the lads he was called Pluto. His type of slow gait always disquiets, then impresses boys. Mr Williams broadened this effect by wearing a huge black oilskin hat. He wore this in all weathers. This was because he lived in an expectation of rain that ran through our communal mood as powerfully as lust through the thoughts of Freud. It also did something for his morale. The leg fractures had reduced the length of his bottom half and he wanted something to add a little to the top. It had its effect. If you had done anything at all out of line you would feel guiltier after being stared at by Mr Williams' deep, dark eyes from beneath that wrinkled canopy.

As often as not he carried a monstrous, thick-bristled brush. He held it stiffly in front of him like a sceptre, and had great skill in using it to push aside the noisy and stun the insolent. The sight of him descending slowly into the cellar, with his hat and brush, and even more slowly ascending, suggested a small divinity keeping in touch with his private domain, conjoint thunderbolt and cleanser, King of the Shadows, product of mutilating ironies: Pluto.

Mr Williams had several reasons for taking a tough line on the troglodytes who, towards the end, were making their soaked way in such numbers down to the cellar he was seriously thinking of asking E.T. to establish blackboards, teachers and other aids below stairs. First, there was the smell of baking pupil, never pleasant. Then there were so many of us sitting on the coke that whenever Mr Williams slid his shovel under the fuel to recharge his boiler he often groaned as he carried the shovel to the furnace, for there would be a boy smiling and sharing the shovel with the coke.

I do not think he minded the smoking very much. It was so dark in the cellar his conscience as a censor was not troubled because he could not see who the individual offenders were. Besides, he did his own smoking down the cellar. He was forbidden to smoke in his own house by his wife, a sharp-eyed woman, brisk in movement, weird in speech, who sold us cocoa at a penny a cup.

It was our language and frivolity that worried Mr Williams. He would sometimes detach an anecdote from the general din and ask the teller to repeat it. When he got the message plain he would lean heavily on his broom, panting, as if ready to faint. In particular he noted my loud and frequent rides on this roundabout of indecency. I was, after all, one of his denomination. Being in the cellar at all, smoking and scrimshanking, meant that I was halfway to hell. He could not, as a deacon, see me make the whole trip.

So, one morning he acted. The cellar population was at a new peak. It had poured with rain all the way from home to school. A few dawdles under dripping eaves and ruptured water-pipes had given the rain clear access to vest and pants. With the cellar tactic available, only dupes and dedicated scholars made their way to the assembly hall and classrooms. The cellar walls were bulging. The stove, clogged by some young technician eager to mask his identity if we were interrupted, was belching a lungful. The fags were going down at top rate. We heard a voice bawl from the entrance to the cellar, 'Upstairs, please!' The bubble of talk continued for half a minute. A few eyes peered through the blue gloom, but there was no real concern.

There was a boy sitting next to me who had just been fitted out with new glasses by the municipal clinic. The glasses had given him extraordinarily sharp sight. He gave us long accounts of what new depth of vision meant to a boy. He was something of a voyeur, being physically timid. The domestic bathing habits of the region were careless, and this boy, with his gift of stealth and piercing sight, had seen many girls and women soaping and swilling themselves in their fireside baths. He was probably a liar as well as a spy, for there was a bizarre note in many of his descriptions. He was not at ease on the cokes and he probably made up these stories to make himself feel more comfortable. He had inspired many boys to try their own eye at this window-watching, and they had been beaten by husbands and brothers who had been keeping a loose guard over their privacy. Not having been fitted out with special aids by the clinic, they had probably pressed too hard and too long against the kitchen windows and drawn attention to themselves.

I heard the boy with the glasses say: 'That's the boss. That's E.T. standing by the entrance, shouting "Upstairs, please".' He repeated the message three or four times. There were guffaws from boys, who thought this must be the end of some complicated joke whose beginning they had missed. For most of us

'Upstairs, please' had one connotation only, eager passion, and the boy with the glasses was urged to begin again.

He repeated his warning. In sections the boys ceased to talk and chuckle. Fags were dowsed on the damp coke. I paid no attention. There was no sign of E.T. He must have been standing on the cellar steps, repelled by the fuming reek from our cavern. The boy with the glasses had probably been fitted by the clinic with means to see round corners. Or, sitting on cokes, on top of all his experiences at windows on bathday, might have driven him off the hinge.

I was the last to keep talking, waving my still lighted cigarette in the air to thicken my points. I thought that the silence was a tribute to the quality of the story I was telling. It was a good moment. I did not care whether E.T. was on the cellar steps or anywhere else. The night before at the Welfare Hall the pornographers had introduced me to a broad catalogue of jests about honeymoon couples. They covered every aspect of farce revealed by the bedroom pioneers of our kind. With this kind of material, I thought, enough rainy mornings and the tolerance of Mr Williams, I would become the King of the Cellar. I was even composing a limerick about cokes to recite at my coronation, a light-weight bard of lubricity, a small but not unworthy Rabelais. The tale was coming to an end. I took an especially deep drag at my fag to get a little extra swing into the peroration.

The story was about a honeymoon couple who stay in their darkened chamber for several days, without pause for food or air. At the end the man has been driven by indulgence into an extreme of emaciation and debility. He gets out of bed to let in some light. He goes up with the blind. I thought I had given a pretty rich rendering of the saga, but mine was the only guffaw that greeted its climax. My companions were as silent and grave as jurors. I felt annoyed.

'Up with the blind. He went up with the blind. The poor bloke had shot his bolt. Too weak to hold the blind down. Can't you see that?'

'He's here,' said the boy with the glasses.

I looked towards the door. E.T. stood there, his mouth adroop with rage, his right hand pointing at my cigarette, his head craning forward as if he had been concentrating on the final details of the honeymoon story. Mr Williams stood at the side of E.T., the business end of his brush covering his face. He looked like a medieval executioner in the service of a king or judge. I heard a voice behind me whisper that Mr Williams was going to fell us systematically as we climbed the steps.

'Upstairs, please!' said E.T. 'To my room.'

We filed up the steps. E.T. touched my arm. 'You'll come in last. You were the last to fall silent in that hell-hole. So you'll be the last to get your punishment.'

I waited for the other boys to pass me and brought up at the end of the procession. I was not displeased. I had heard that E.T. had a slight hernia. I guessed that he would go at the first dozen victims with a wild zeal. By the time he got to me, the thirty-fourth flogee, he would, I thought, have split his cane or be crouched in distress.

Neither thing happened. His weapon was a walking stick of first-class make, and he had kept a finely swinging arm in reserve for me. He had me walking around like a duck for days on end. On the twelfth stroke I was convinced I would have to look for my privates on the back pages of the *Police Gazette*.

That beating was his most passionate assertion of the values he cherished most in personal conduct: no dereliction in one's classroom duties, no smoking on piles of coke, no bandying of tales that put the sex act in a comic light. He watched me closely after that. Every time I turned up late I was clobbered. And I was often late. The hills were steep, the breakfasts perfunctory and my general mood in favour of a leaden stillness.

On the sharper slopes my big bag of best leather dragged me back like the Erl King. And daily I dawdled to check on any drama that might be developing behind my back. In the complete absence of power, wealth and bliss, I at least wanted to know. I wanted to do the whole trip around the seeable facts of other people's lives.

That long village street helped me in this. People tended to live operatically, in shouts. The withdrawn, the secluded, were few. There was little of the sly, terrifying madness that simmers on a low flame in many other places. Our freaks were forthright and friendly. Most of the front doors, whose doorsteps were a part of the sidewalk, were open as often as not. This was to allow for the violent eviction of nuisances without damage to the woodwork, or for the entrance of miracles, an event rarely on the timetable. The open door also served to reduce the endemic smell of damp rot that hung about the valley's dwellings, a sad, sweetish smell that would lay flat the liveliest spirit.

It is said that the odour of damp-rotten wood enhances the sense of life's pathetic insistence on loss and separateness. It causes ghosts to materialise and prompts the living to see them. If this is so, we had more ghosts than registered voters, and many councillors believed the ghosts should pay some kind of half-rate to help with the general problems like council housing, and even the need for drier wood to keep the ghosts down.

But the main function of the yawning front door was welcome and easy access. Never did people flow so from house to house. With calamity running at a steady rate, lost jobs, injured bodies, infant mortality, silence and withdrawal were taboo. The closing of a door was like the planting of a tombstone. The drift of nomadic groups into one another's houses was an unguent. It diluted the ulcer juices.

With pointed bayonets and aggressive helmets on every skyline, one wanted constantly the sight and sound of the tribe. Quiet introspection would quickly kill a slum, a ghetto. So we shouted, sang and stared in fascination at the antics of the people up and down the road. From almost every house aspects of the unbelievable came pelting.

So I listened at the open doors and this made a snarl of my progress to school. From the kitchens beyond the passages, bits of wild dialogue would come flying. 'Don't comb your hair into the bloody salad.' 'How many times must I tell you not to use my fretsaw to slice the bread.' I would wait for these themes to be developed. Mostly they were not. An idiom of brittle nervousness prevailed and one sentence was usually enough to use up the oxygen. 'He's sitting there like a mummy and he's giving me the creeps.' 'Don't look at me like that. How was I to know the blade of the hatchet was loose?' 'If I want to sing "Among My Souvenirs" I'll bloody well sing "Among My Souvenirs".'

I would pause invariably on the bridge that divided the town. The river, in spate, was an interesting sight. People threw a lot of their refuse into it, and it was a pastime to identify the various objects that got caught among the large rocks that littered its bed. One morning I saw, floating swiftly to the south, four chickens, two dogs and a man, in that order. That morning I did not get to school at all. I joined a posse that started galloping along the river bank to rescue the chickens and identify the man.

E.T. would wait for me at the top of the school drive, watch in hand, determined to put the disordered fragments of my life into something like shape. Sometimes he would wait for a few more laggards to fall into the net, but most often I was the end of the procession.

I knew the routine. I left my bag in the cloakroom and lay prone on the table in E.T.'s room to wait for the tanning. Quite frequently some bit of business held him up on the way to his study and I would have a long wait. It is a curious feeling to be stretched out on your stomach on a mahogany table staring at a complete edition of the *Encyclopaedia Britannica* in the bookshelf opposite. Not as purging or constructive as yoga, but a start in that direction.

The walking stick he used on me and other obstinate offenders was special. It was a relic of the days he had spent abroad as a young man. He had, it appeared, been a great walker and had tramped his way through all the Swiss cantons. Nailed to the stick were small silver medallions bearing the name of the town or village in which they had been bought: Berne, Lucerne, Davos, Evian.

E.T.'s aim with the stick was not consistent and he rarely laid the same stretch of medallions on me twice running. By the time the beatings finished my buttocks were imprinted with

a tourist's guide to the whole Swiss territory, and it probably
had something to do with my interest in foreign languages.

*

Standing before E.T.'s front gate on my way to the tea en-
gagement I found myself reluctant to push the gate open. E.T.'s
house was large, solid and imposing, as were the houses on
either side, big-windowed with doors that struck me as top
quality, richly stained glass breaking up the stretches of expen-
sive wood, a piece of old Versailles against the general archi-
tectural background of the valley.

I asked a passing man the time. Half past four. I was supposed
to have been knocking at the door fifteen minutes before. E.T.
came out of the house, his watch in his hand.

'Late again,' he said. 'Come in.'

I followed E.T. into the house. He took me into the parlour,
the largest room in a private house I had ever seen. The furni-
ture was built for giants. The armchairs seemed to be the size of
our kitchen sofa, which we regarded as an article of majesty.
The predominant colour was dark red, which I found gloomy.
It was not helped by large photographs of elderly Welsh people,
two women caught in a mood of heavy brooding but beautiful
in a sullen, life-defeated way. Between the pictures of the two
women were portraits of two men. They were heavily bearded,
one beard black, the other grey, and had fierce eyes. They were,
in most particulars, very alike, turned out of a mould of inces-
sant labour and raking moral gunnery. They had put a life-
time's stamina into their mixed entry of rejections. They did
not make me feel less nervous. They were well inside our hard
core of forbidding severity. I took them to be the parents of
E.T. and his wife.

Mrs E.T. came in with the tea. She was a genial woman, wear-
ing immensely thick glasses. The tea-set was of silver, glittering
and ornate. It was heavy and pulled Mrs E.T.'s body painfully
forward. But the thing gave her pride which showed all over
her face, despite the hidden, inscrutable eyes. She would have

carried in that rich, crippling load if it had pulled her on to her face.

I had seen very little of silver. There had been a set of communion vessels in the chapel I had attended, but they had been disappointingly lacklustre. The caretaker was an extreme sectarian, against ecclesiastical pomp in any shape or form, and polished the vessels only when driven and threatened by the deacons. It was found later that he was allergic to the smell of metal polish and he was replaced by a man who throve on the smell of Brasso, and did not mind having the chapel gloom relieved from time to time by a glint of loveliness.

Another owner of silver had been my Uncle Oscar, a cantankerous jeweller who lived in a place called Mountain Ash. He had what he described as a cache of old silver behind his shop, and he had once shown it to my father and myself as if it were the treasure of Sutton Hoo. It had looked dim to me and did not compare with E.T.'s splendid tea things.

Uncle Oscar had specialised in engraving silver coffin plates. Towards the end of his life his hands had become useless with rheumatoid arthritis and his mind clouded by a raging misanthropy. He was one of the first people to receive gold injections for his arthritis. They did not work and when gold jumped in price in the 1930s he tried to sell his body for its gold contents. There were no takers. It was thought that not even gold would retain its integrity in a body as acidulous as his.

He claimed to have been part-inventor of the Mills bomb. This claim deepened his general loneliness. The puritans hated him for his jewels and the fillip he gave to ostentation. The pacifists despised him for his contribution to bombing. He told me shortly before he died that he was delighted to have helped in the creation of a weapon that delivered mischief on a broad, indiscriminate front. The last coffin plate he engraved was his own. It was beautiful, its lettering well beyond Gothic in its endless twirls. Between perversity and stiffness of limb he was no longer capable of a plain script.

During all the years I knew him his language mounted into a wild, unhappy profanity. From every sentence hung an Indian temple of carnal imagery. He was the perfect alliance of Timon of Athens and D. H. Lawrence of Eastwood, with a few metaphors about the stuffing of animals, remembered from a brief spell with a taxidermist, thrown in to stiffen the mixture.

As I sat there in E.T.'s parlour, looking at my diffident image in the lid of the muffin-dish, I wondered what effect Oscar would have had on E.T., his wife and his four ancestors in their picture-frames. I looked at the eyes of the man with the black beard. It would not have surprised me to hear him telling Oscar to move up and join him.

Mrs E.T. was a cook of quality. I pitched into the muffins, scones, toast, cream cakes. I ate on behalf of all the under-privileged and I could hear my stomach cracking down the sides. The non-stop stuffing of the mouth also excused me from making any reply to E.T., who was in top form and spate. He was giving me a list of men he had known in his life who had come out of villages and homes twice as crouched as mine, passed through Oxford and gone on to golden careers. Through the titbits I grunted and nodded, blinking my eyes in agreement but without any faith that my luck would be consistent with that of E.T.'s acquaintances.

But my eyes in the main were fixed on E.T.'s wife. I had never seen her in any private light before. She had lived a fairly chipped life. Her father had been a saddler in the West Welsh town of Ammanford, a place largely Welsh-speaking and complacent about itself. It manages to imprint a great stamp of confidence on its children.

Mrs E.T. grew up with a soprano voice of great power and money enough to have it trained. She went to one of the London music colleges and stayed with one of her relatives, a dairyman whom she helped in his business. She developed some sort of painter's colic spraying white eggs with brown paint to make them seem fresher to the London clients, who had a fetish in favour of brown eggs. She studied voice in the same class as Eva Turner, the great Turandot, and Mrs E.T.'s voice in timbre and power had exactly the same quality as Miss Turner's.

The sopranos of that time must have been nourished on the

dream of having a go at Turandot. A long and painful series of operations on her eyes for the removal of minute growths broke the continuity of her training. That and marriage kept her out of the opera house. Whatever Mrs E.T. sang, arias of mad operatic heroines or simple lullabies, she would always make it sound like '*In questa reggia*'. I based a large part of my technique as a boy alto on hers and it did me no good. My notes landed on the audience like hurled cabers and made programme arrangers nervous.

In her husband's first years at the school she often came along to sing at the school concerts. The hugeness of her voice had caused E.T. to advise her to stick to the softer type of lyric, but it made no difference. She was fond of a clutch of songs all dealing with Welsh exiles returning from fat enterprises in places like Rio, Buenos Aires, Melbourne, Hong Kong to tiny villages in the slate valleys of North Wales, asking for no greater privilege than to be buried in some gaunt, hill-top graveyard alongside their parents and childhood friends. These songs would have sounded well given a low, crooning treatment. But either through nerves or some awkward acoustic Mrs E.T., from the first notes on, sounded as if she were jumping on us from the summit of some great despair or rage.

If the people coming back from the sunlit places like Rio to settle in the graveyards of their natal places sounded like her they were coming back only to disturb. It was interesting to watch the effect of her voice on the rows of boys sitting to listen to her in the main hall of our school. Many of them, boys with ear-bones worn to paper thinness by undernourishment, or the labours of Onan, would cause a small riot by trying to move swiftly out of range.

I cleared the piles of food in all the silver dishes, and rounded the meal off with so many cups of tea E.T. looked at me as if wondering whether to call for a vote of thanks or an autopsy.

When the meal was over, Mrs E.T. smiled at me, suggesting, I thought, that after what I had tucked away I would not know hunger for at least a term. She said, 'I remember you singing a song called "The Blackbird" a long time ago. A nice song.'

D

I remembered it. It had been one of my favourites. It was about a harpist entranced into silence by the song of this bird. 'Oh, blackbird, I list to thy singing, My harp for a while shall be still.' The song had suited my pitch and throbbing style, and I had given it all the cannon in my fort. With that volume the blackbird would not only have been out of its tree but bald as well.

Mrs E.T. came closer to me. She looked at me intently, with great sympathy. 'You were a nice-looking boy then,' she said. 'I thought of that song and the way you looked then came back to me as clean as a pin. Isn't it funny?'

I stood up, shaking with shame and an impending sense of surfeit. I was aware of the gauntness of my cheeks, the stoop of my back, and I agreed with the verdict of Mrs E.T. I had declined dramatically in grace. If I had been pulled over the threshold of manhood by a team of alley cats I would not have looked worse. Still, I had put my words together well on the examination papers, and I was shortly going to leave the valley for more than one night.

E.T. went to a desk in the corner of the room. He took out a book which I did not recognise to be a cheque-book. He wrote me a cheque for twenty-five pounds.

'This will help,' he said. 'It's a loan, not a gift. When you finish at Oxford you'll be well set-up. You can pay it back then with ease. When your body straightens a bit and your character hardens you could make a lot of yourself. Don't hide from people. You will, but try not to. You have many dark emotions. Blench them. Restore God to your little acre, smoke less and if, when you come to planning your honours course and have a choice between the modern and medieval periods, don't go for the Middle Ages. They'll be bad for you. As untidy as you are.'

He shook my hand and gave me the cheque. I thought that was the end of the business. But he added, 'You know I've watched out for you over the years.'

'Yes, sir,' I said. 'Thank you, sir.' And I left the house.

*

I pressed forward with getting the overcoat from Mr Warlow, the tailor, for which Mr Metcalfe had paid. My father was convinced that the overcoat was going to make up for a lot of past defeats.

'This overcoat will impress the English, make them less bossy. Pity you didn't have a more dashing tailor than Warlow. A moody and perverse man, Warlow, with no belief in clothes or clients.'

Mr Warlow made me the coat. He did not believe in preliminary fitting. A quick run-over with the tape and Mr Warlow's long traffic with fashion would do the rest. My father and my brother Dil were doubtful. 'His best customers,' said Dil, 'have been gnomes.'

A large group assembled to see me put the coat on for the first time, for between the ascension of a local boy to Oxford and the sight of so much new fabric the occasion was regarded as pretty glossy.

When the garment fell into place there was silence. My father stared at Mr Warlow as if he were the last instalment in some long purchase of perplexity. The coat came to within an inch or two of the floor. The buttons, of prodigious size, seemed to come down just as far, as if afraid to let the fabric make the long journey south on its own. Mr Warlow did not seem to have taken my stoop into consideration, and the great hoop of collar looked down at my neck either with contempt or just thoughtfully.

I made an instant demand, backed up by my father, who had got hold of Mr Warlow's major scissors and was waving it threateningly, that the coat be shortened by a foot and Mr Warlow hanged. Mr Warlow was offended, said the coat was the best thing he had ever made and added that he was prepared to defend it to the death. My father, working the scissors, said he might not have long to wait.

Mr Warlow explained that the coat had been the last length of one bolt and he had not wanted any left over. I expected him to add that the buttons had been the shields of small volunteers in some forgotten war. But he did not say this. He seemed to regard the buttons as normal.

Then came the campaign to assure me, to make me accept the coat as part of a new billowing destiny. The campaign was led by Mr Metcalfe, who was a friend of Mr Warlow and favourable to anything that kept the body hidden. Some of the thinkers in the Welfare Hall said that in that length of coat I looked like the last of the Romanoffs, a family that went in for vast surtouts. Others pointed out that any attempt to alter the style would alter the magnificent symmetry of the buttons, which the more deprived and suggestible were already beginning to worship and rub for luck. Dil said there might be some way of tying my neck to the collar to make the whole thing hang a little more reasonably.

So I settled for it. On the morning of my departure for the ancient university I marched down the hill to the coach station feeling like an emperor and looking like a cross between Sam Weller and a shrouded dwarf. It was a considerable procession. All my brothers were there. Nana, as always reserved in her public emotions, had waved goodbye to me and gone instantly back into the house to take up her everlasting tasks.

At the head of the parade were Dil and John, bearing Mr Metcalfe's trunk reverently, as if it were the covenanted ark. Behind them came Mr Metcalfe, stroking the trunk as if he agreed with them. Various neighbours joined in. They were keeping in trim for the next funeral or thought our turn-out to be a nice change from the demonstrations the voters were always organising against the pinch-penny tactics of the Government.

Mr Warlow was one of the party that saw me off. He kept fingering my coat and saying that he had never handled or sold a more solid bit of stuff. It was as heavy as lead. Between it, the excitement and solemnity, I was whacked. I had to be helped over the last ten yards to the coach.

It had rained heavily in the night, but, for once, I did not study the hillside for any trace of new, menacing freshets. Even as the coach conductor was reaching for my ticket I fell into a deep sleep that lasted until Lydney, on the borders of Gloucester-shire. When I awoke I was exactly midway between the valley and Oxford, the conductor told me. My whole being divided under the impact of that fact and it was never to be the same again.

2

And there were those millions of broken moons

I passed through Oxford in three years, one stupor and four and a half suits. Mr Warlow died before he got to the trousers.

Had I been a Venusian I would not have made smaller contact with the place. The high and ancient walls provided an acoustic that was unbearably sharp. The speech of the townspeople reached me in the form of a yelp. That of the students was so languid I had to keep my ear incessantly close to them to gather anything of their drift at all.

The average height of the undergraduates I found disconcerting. In the valley the average height of our men was about five feet six. We accepted that. History had meant us to be short and history had had its way. The aboriginal Celts had stunted themselves by long spells of hiding under outcrops of low rock. Their descendants, still out of luck, had happened to be on hand in places where there was coal to be dug. The abundance of men of over six feet in height at Oxford, all serene with health and strength, startled me.

I found myself walking up and down the High Street peering into beautiful silken, many-coloured waistcoats at the latitude of the navel. Time and again I looked up to find a pair of upper-class eyes staring down at me as if they had just seen their first mole. In relation to these lofty blooms I saw myself as little better than greenfly. I met no one who could sing in tune and the lack of close harmony hurt like hunger.

I spent only the third of my three years living in college. To this virtual segregation from the collegiate body I owed what peck of sanity remained to me when I left Oxford. My first lodgings were at the end of the Cowley Road which stood out even at the close of the Industrial Revolution, a deadly place where a man called Morris set himself to making the first cheap cars in Britain, and I never walked down that dreary highway without feeling that Morris had begun an insuperable mischief.

My landlord and landlady were a peculiar pair, greyly obtuse and medieval in their responses. Their thinking had about it the rocky peace of the pyramids. They were traditionalists to within a breath of coma. Their heads were stuffed with old *Daily Mails* and every time they turned an ear to the quick, subversive tumble of my words you could hear the Mafeking headlines rustle.

The food they gave me had a brutal air about it. Bacon and eggs going down in grease for a third and terrible time. For lunch slices of cold beef that suggested less than any other kinds of meat that they had ever belonged to life. This was followed by two portions of a dark brown Swiss Roll. I would not touch them. They reappeared the next day and the next day. Dust formed on them. On gayer days I would write things with my finger on the dusty beef and cake. When they next hove to I would pass the time on reading yesterday's message. The food was not altogether to blame. A chronic hypertension that came in with the midwife, an absence of exercise, smoking too much and a way of bending dramatically over my books had made a joke of my digestion. Any food assimilated by my system had run the longest gauntlet in the history of the alimentary tract.

So, I withdrew from the conventional breakfast and lunch. I explained to the landlady that my family fortunes had come crashing. My father, through misguided loyalty, had hung on too long to his holdings in ten of the valley's pits and had been wiped out as a result. He had sent a personal courier to Oxford to tell me to draw my horns in. This, if true, would have been the shortest operation ever connected with horns. It was a good lie, passionately told. It had me in tears, but the landlady stayed as cool and sullen as her beef. I felt sorry for my father and had a wish to send him and the ten pits a message urging them not to lose faith, that capitalism still had a lot of fire in its belly, still a lot of gold for its votaries. The letter would not have perplexed him any more than the general drift of life in that age.

I switched from bacon and egg to biscuits and quantities of tea that drove the last of my digestive juices into the tundra. I left the house each day for morning lectures as hungry as Asia, with a stomach rumble that confused three lecturers and silenced a fourth.

A rejection of food was a theme of the whole experience. Many people fell under the spell of college dining halls with their portraits of ancient dons and eminent graduates. The spell did not work with me. Standing gowned in a quadrangle among a group of gowned men, waiting for the bell in the college chapel to toll the eating hour gave me a sense of strangeness that made my jaw droop. We always seemed to sit too many to a bench and I normally qualified for the end seat, being a hell of a chap for letting other people get in before me, and most of my fellow diners were aggressively superior lads who were only too glad to let me do so. When the Principal and his aides filed in everyone stood and quite often when we sat down again my companions had spread themselves and there was no bench beneath me. At the price of a few rattled spinal discs and a little bruise I gained a reputation as a buffoon.

The meal got off to a bad start with a grace spoken in Latin. A loathing of ritual was the marrow of my ideological bones, and I often annoyed my table-mates by looking around at the roomful of devoutly lowered heads. My experience of preprandial prayer and non-family eating had been small.

During the long industrial struggles of my childhood that

had brought mining to a halt for months on end I and my fel-
lows had been skimpily fed in local vestries out of public
funds. These feasts were called 'soup kitchens' and were every
bit as rough as their names. They were attended by little cere-
mony. Our first supervisor had tried to dignify the occasion. He
was a benevolent man. He was full of love for everyone but
had a poor sense of timing. He had itched for years with a wish
to say grace before a meal, and he thought we might afford him
his last chance. He tried it four or five times before falling back
into silence. He gestured us to our feet and began his thanks.
He gave a perfunctory nod at God, then went on to name and
praise all the miners' unions in Europe that had contributed to
the fine quality of the soup. Then he would pay tribute to local
benefactors who had come across with the odd bob. By this time
his voice would be flattened beneath the champing of our
famished teeth into the bread, and shouts from the people
making the soup in huge cauldrons in the backyard that if the
oration droned on for much longer the stuff would have
evaporated.

Conversation in the soup kitchen was sparse: snarled de-
mands for bread or beans, little more. But conversation in the
college dining hall was loud, constant and, to my ears, un-
reasonable. The high-pitched pecking accent of the Southern
English pained my mastoid bone. The ideas expressed caused me
no less dismay. The talkers divided into two factions. There
were those who revelled in the orthodox piety that gave the col-
lege its tone of chirpy altruism. Many of these were members
of the Oxford Group, followers of Dr Frank Buckman, pro-
ponents of a bright-eyed evangelism of which Dr Billy Graham
is the current major torch.

They claimed that they had surrendered all power and per-
sonal decision. God, they claimed, took them by the hand first
thing in the morning and led them through the day. I believed
this in part. They had a genuinely mesmerised look. They smiled
ceaselessly and delighted in touching one on the hand, the
shoulder. It took me a year to realise that their smile was sin-
cere, in no way sardonic, their touch asensual. They made it

plain they cared about me. They looked at my suspicious eyes, listened incredulously to my distempered tongue and urged me to fall in behind Buckman before it was too late. They sensed in every breath of my being a whiff of smouldering faggot and their hands were outstretched to haul me aboard their band-wagon of passive serenity.

I attended several of their meetings. They were mass-confessionals given to verbal orgasm, an exposure of sores of the sort favoured by such sects as the Pentecostals. The pivot of their jousts was a young woman of loose habits who fell from grace week after week and was spiritually restored in time for the meeting. She described her lapses with rushes of detail that kept the room packed and the faith aflame. She was a pavement labourer of radiant charm. She attracted me. Her voice was deep, her arm movements ample. The metaphors flashed like fish through her brisk saga of lapse and regeneration. But she never gave me a glance. In that circle of upstanding Christian paladins I ranked as little higher than a dark pagan Toby jug. Which was a pity. Had I been drawn fully into that fold I might have lived to walk forward to receive the benediction of Dr Graham.

The other faction in the table talk were the political zealots. This was my first contact with High Toryism. I was impressed by its assurance, bewildered by its flavour. In the valley a seam of socialist dogma took up nine-tenths of the mental space. The need for equality was accepted as being as urgent as the need for air, milk, speech. Anyone found truckling to authority or embracing the *status quo* was rejected as a freak. Insurrectionary fanatics podded like peas.

It never occurred to me that I would one day find a matching set of furious spites. I did when I first listened to those fellow diners. Many of them had spent vacations in Germany, and they had come back full of praise for the plans and notions of the then emergent Hitler. The stables of pacifism and decadence, said these lads, were in for a scrubbing and you could see the bristles sticking out of their every syllable.

Every sentence they uttered had me choking on my meat.

With the first few letters of the alphabet I had absorbed the view that militant nationalism is a dangerous obscenity. I told them that if they expressed these ideas to an average group of miners the shock would bleach the coal they dug. That set the diners off. Forks of menace came close to my eyes. The miners had come out of the industrial disputes of the twenties with a vile reputation. They had become the bogeymen of all the secure and uncrumpled communities of the land.

One of the pro-Nazis, an aquiline fellow who made a regular breakfast of loathing on toast, told me that he had seen it announced somewhere that the Welsh stock had been heavily drenched by infusions of Jewish and Negro blood. I felt pleased, enlarged. I shook myself to give him a glug of tainted plasm.

From Bodicea, the Icenian queen, to Aneurin Bevan, of Ebbw Vale, we had been devoted to the task of discolouring the substance of Aryan supremacy. The Welsh sang so much, not out of any sincere respect for harmony but to muffle the racket made by their single function, belting hell out of the British Raj and decent conventions. It was only a matter of time before my assegai got to work on the head of the college principal, and I started a bonfire of prayer-mats collected from my Semitic and Arab allies beneath the college chapel.

These meals were not for me. Even without the ideological thickets through which I trudged in solitude, they were too long. At home one sat down to a single dish. In the fastest time one got it down and cleared off. But in this new type of feast the soup was just the opening shot and the rest of the battle was pretty dismal. I got a medical note and took it to one of the college officials. It said I was suffering from some kind of Celtic ulcer that struck early and never relented. It might well have been true. Around about the age of six I began to regard food as a nuisance and have never ceased to do so. I was excused from obligatory dining. I would sidle up the High Street, buy a couple of burning pies from the transport café I went to on the night of my first visit to Oxford to be interviewed by the Head of my college. I would nibble at the searing pastry with startled lips and a heart to match.

One night the aquiline man caught me with a pie in either hand. I heard him say that with this equipment of pasties I was probably on my way to some sinister kind of North African celebration. 'God is threatened, deserts widen and Gordon is no more.' Blowing on my pies to cool them, I agreed.

Intellectually the going was no less peculiar. The lectures at the Taylorean Institute, donated, I was told, by the omnilateral arms-vendor, Basil Zaharoff, to commemorate the dead Oxonians of World War I, were languid. The lecture rooms rustled with a whispered gentility that reminded one of the rubberoid surface of the Institute's floors, which muted shoes and brought one's sense of identity and direction dangerously low.

My teachers at school had done their job with a grating urgency. They had kept us at it like huntsmen. Their voices had had the precise quality of hallooing bugles. Every fact was a scent, and we were told to bark our respect for it. Learning and teaching had for them no especial beauty. They were doing a first-aid job, pushing us up a lift shaft of academic grace, from a ghastly underworld to a lighted surface.

Among my college mentors the whole temperature dropped. There were weeks on end when I wearied utterly of lectures and stayed away, keeping fast to my lodgings. After one such period of withdrawal, I was visited by the Principal of the college who thought I had died or fled. Only once did my mind flare with interest. A woman lecturer, a querulous lady, was giving us a broad analysis of Baudelaire. She expelled me from the room for failing to take notes.

At the beginning of the third term I was supposed to fix myself up with a tutor. This I failed to do, through a mixture of ignorance and diffidence. When I appeared at the term's end before the committee of dons who were to adjudicate my progress, they were curious but not angry about this gap in my routine. I explained that I was very shy and had no wish to bother anyone. This was quite true. I have always tended to become paralysed at the prospect of making contact with a fresh person. I could, without a qualm, have spent my life in a single doorway, nodding at people, and that only on effusive days, no more.

The Principal said that the tutorial system was the rudder of the University system, and it was reckless of me to go tossing about in a boat of my own, and said that when I returned from the vacation he would study my conduct with sympathetic curiosity. The other members of the committee looked at me as if they had already marked me down as one of the few people who had a State Scholarship and the reflexes of an imbecile. They were right. Whatever lumbered me with my present set of reflexes is a half-read mystery. The original set, the good, sane ones, slipped through a thousand fissures in my quaking days. Most of the people I meet seem to be in the same wagon, caught in a mesh of sly, indecipherable idiocies.

In my second year things brightened a little on the lodging front. I moved away from the gloomy Cowley suburb and glad to go. Living in the suburb was a young man from the valley a little older than myself. He had no connection with the University. He was a barman in one of the city's rougher pubs, but when not serving in this place he would walk gravely about in an academic gown and an armful of books that would have broken any arm not strengthened by constant work on the ale pumps. Whenever I saw him approach I would leap into alleys and doorways. I did not wish to see or feel the raw flesh of hopelessness inside his fantasy.

The new lodgings were in Headington, a high place on the way to Shotover Hill, a walk beloved of Shelley during his short and bitter conflict with the orthodox crustaceans of his University days. Groups of devout fellow students would come up to visit me and escort me on long healthful walks to the top of the hill, coaxing me into sweeter thoughts and attitudes less farouche, heading me off from the sulphur holes. They got no further with me than they did with Shelley.

I shared my lodgings with a notable man and remarkable linguist and musician, called John Wynne Roberts. He was from a village three miles or so from mine in the valley. His father was a bankrupt draper, ruined by the second of the great coal strikes, but who seemed to have come through the experience with a fair walletful.

Wynne had come up to Magdalen College to read Italian and failed to get on with his Italian tutor, who had become peculiar after too many years of holding the lamp for Dante. Wynne switched to English and his tutor this time was the theologian, poet and writer of children's tales, C. S. Lewis. Wynne's link with him was brittle. Until the age of eighteen his parents had forced him into being the regular champion at competitions in religious knowledge. Ask him the distance between any two places named in the Bible and he would snap back the answer as if he had paced it out that very week. He could recite the genealogies of the tribes of Israel as if they were related to him by marriage. He had sickened of it. He was a refugee from every book in the two Testaments except the Gospel according to St Matthew. He kept that in his conscience because of Bach's Passion which he could sing right through. Had he not wished to avoid creating an impression of instability he would have treated English as he had Italian and moved on to something else.

They were happy lodgings. The landlady gave us mixed-grill breakfasts which saw me at least right to the end of the day. We kept hunger down with tobacco. We both smoked to excess. Between a smoke-screen and an addiction to the cinema we were rarely in sight. Wynne had a good collection of Wagner records and a large gramophone which complicated our journey to the bus-stop at the end of term. Over that whole year is the flavour of grilled kidneys and the sound of the *Siegfried Idyll*.

My luck with tutors was little better than Wynne's. My Spanish tutor was a small man with many malignant undertones. He hated England. He was, he made it quite plain, dying of disgust and regarded me as having been paid to come along and finish him off. He had been a friend of Lorca and had a good name as a poet in Spain. He survived to become one of Franco's laureate bards. He was passionately monarchist, Catholic and nervous. Feeling the cold he conducted his tutorials in a kind of greenhouse. This did not help. Reading a fairly incoherent essay in Spanish and feeling like a cucumber at the same time does not bring out the best in me.

Had I planned my honours course a little more wisely my troubles with him might have been fewer. I had to choose one of three periods for specialist study: the Middle Ages, the Golden Age, comparable in time and quality to our own Elizabethan Age, and the Modern Period, comparable in time and quality to nobody else's modern period. I sought no one's advice and if ever a man needed advice it was I. My aptitude for wrong decisions has never flagged. From every choice I have made a doom dangles.

I recalled that E.T. had warned me against taking up with the Middle Ages, so I chose the Middle Ages. E.T. felt that I would not make a good medievalist. My tutor knew so and said so in some of the hardest Spanish I have ever heard. He detested the Middle Ages, and I sometimes felt that his knowledge of the period's literature was only a short ballad ahead of mine. His own special field was the poetry of Gongora, a seventeenth-century poet and one of Europe's most subtle and affected writers. After long immersion in that kind of delicacy I could see my tutor wince as he helped me unearth the stony banalities in the chronicles that told us of Wilfred the Hairy, Roderick the Rough, Sancho the Sod and the rest.

One of the texts we studied was a long verse-narrative *The Book of Splendid Love*, by a lecherous friar called Juan Ruiz, a contemporary of Chaucer. The poem showed Ruiz, whose cassock must have been in a state of constant disarray, seducing his way through numberless mountain villages, flashing like a mole through the sexual cellarage of every lonely female life, a cadger of genius, master of minor chicane and major fornications.

My tutor loathed the poem, reviled its repetitions, its sniggering anti-clericalism and brazen amorality. On one occasion I was droning through an appreciation of Ruiz, hinting that I found him a pretty sharp fellow and comparing him with certain Welsh divines who had gone through life in much the same way, but at lower altitudes and lacking the final, lyrical

impulse to leave a long, frank poem on the subject of com-
plaisant women behind them. I ended the essay flatly by saying
that I had always regarded a theological obsession as one of the
busier branches of the libido.

This brought my tutor to the boil. He was already in distress
with an attack of hay-fever which he had contracted from one
of the plants in the greenhouse. He had had a common cold
from the moment he landed in England, and he regarded the
hay-fever as a black and logical bonus deserved by anyone who
came to live among Protestants and frequent river-mists. He
rose from his seat in a fine Andalusian despair. He walked
around the greenhouse, sniffing at every plant in turn, trying to
track down the one that had set his sinuses flaring and his eyes
streaming. He was also muttering that just one more knock at
theology and the ideal of chastity out of me and I'd be winding
up in the same pot as his early tomatoes. That was my last
tutorial with him and we parted with an almost unbearable de-
light in the conviction that the anguish was over, that we would
never, in any reasonable context, be burdened with each other
again.

The tutorials were carried on entirely in Spanish. There must
still be people along the Banbury Road in Oxford who remem-
ber a wild-looking youth asking them to talk in English and
restore him to a sense of reality. I have never spoken a foreign
language without an intolerable sense of taking part in the
worst kind of amateur dramatics. I have always gaped at the
effrontery of people who claim to see a virtue in a multiplicity
of tongues. Anyone who struggles to revive a language that is
dying gracefully and without pain is guilty of a most harmful
treason.

Take Catalan. That was a language right down on the floor.
But three men on a twenty-year drinking bout had not heard the
news of the language's death. They kept talking it and they
were the nucleus of the revival, making the issue of Catalan a
first-class nuisance in the already bedevilled life of Spain.
Awareness and eloquence are the twin horns of our direst pox,
and a witless pride in one's mother tongue sharpens them both.

E

One day we will choose to sit in a cave, shut up and stay alive.

At the end of my third term at Oxford something happened to relieve the financial ache. My brothers and sisters had been sending oxygen down the line, but not enough to rid the situation of its suggestions of black farce. My father could not help. The Government had cut his unemployment pay by ten per cent in a joint attempt to save the pound and sink my father. Now and then I called into the office of the college and made statements about the payment of my bills so inscrutable the Bursar must have thought me a vagrant con-man who had dropped in to take Oxford for a pound or two.

Then an organisation called Miners' Welfare made me a grant that doubled my income and halved my chances of immediate madness. These grants usually went to people who had themselves worked in pits. I had never done so. I had lived on the lip of a pit and had never been down one and would, if given the chance, have preferred the gibbet. But my father had been a miner. He had been out of work so long it took serious research to make his connection with the industry clear, but they made it.

They summoned me to an interview in London. I had never been to the place before. A group of schoolboys in our village had gone on an outing to the Wembley Exhibition in 1924, and had come back with tales of imperial marvels. For months they walked our streets as grave as Academicians, looking as experienced as Livingstone. I missed that trip. My brother went and returned laden with gifts: a sixpenny tray commemorating Wembley for my sister Nana, and for me a book, also worth sixpence, of tales by Edgar Allan Poe which I, a gay necrophile of eleven, found utterly to my taste. As a bit of supplementary solace I was given threepence to see a film. It was *Robin Hood,* with Douglas Fairbanks as Hood and Wallace Beery as Richard Lionheart.

I sat in the darkness of the cinema (its registered name was The Grand), entranced by Sherwood, archery, banditry and the sight of Fairbanks, all boldness and buttocks, vaulting over castle walls, clutching in my hands the volume of Poe, rich with a new sense of culture. One caption from the film stuck in my mind: 'See they have splintered their lances. Ever a good omen for Huntingdon.'

For a long time afterwards I would stop suddenly in front of people and come out with this line, slowly and clearly. No one made head or tail of it. Either they thought I was reporting on some aspect of their lives that had grown hopelessly dim, or they put me down as a mad envoy from the little people under the hill.

So I got my first glimpse of London by way of the Miners' Welfare Fund. There are people who, when they arrive in London from the provinces for the first time, find instantly that the place fits. 'This is where I should have been from the start. This is my place. This is the world I never want to leave.' These were not the words I spoke. I am sorry they were not. London seems to invest its residents with a self-importance that must be pleasantly narcotic.

The minute I got off the train my feet seemed to be perched on rolling boulders. And I have never landed there since without a sense of malignant insecurity. My mood has always been that of a man in whose wake I once left the station. He was walking up the ramp that leads into Praed Street. He was with his wife. He was lugging a large, scuffed suitcase. There was a look of crumpled innocence about them both. She was looking around her edgily, without gladness. He pointed at a newspaper poster. It said: 'Nude Blonde Found Strangled In Paddington.'

'See?' said the man. 'They're at it all the time.'

The Underground railway foxed and fretted me from the start. The phobic dislike of holes in the ground and whirring machinery rooted in my origins set me off on the wrong foot. I hung about the platform after a slow descent from ground level, peering at every sign like an anxious Orpheus. I watched the trains that roared out of the tunnel. I saw them but did not believe them. When I had nerved myself to enter the train I drew back at the last moment and got caught in the automatic doors. A sophisticated matron, who must have been the president of the local savate group, booted me into the interior. I cracked my head against the further side. Two travellers helped me to a seat.

I wondered to how many of its users London Transport gave this baptism of blood. I checked on my money, ribs and manhood. I sat there for what seemed like a long year, motionless beneath a seven-layer hood of hysteria, being shuttled from Paddington to a place called Cockfosters. I was convinced that my heart and nerves would be nailed in this posture for ever, rolling beneath London until I was shot as a recurrent nuisance at Cockfosters or Paddington.

I was two hours late for the interview. I was addressed by a very thin aristocratic man. His lung power was low and most of what he said stayed in the back of his head. I bent forward as far as I could and gave my answers very much in the dark. The terror that still stayed on my face after those hours in the Tube must have been taken for eagerness. And some of my answers must have landed in the target area. The aristocrat smiled as he shook my hand at the interview's end. During the tea that followed a friendly official told me that he had made an assessment of my character. That was part of his job, assessing people, assaying the ore of the human specimens who put in for aid. I, he said, was shrewd, a young man with an eye to the main chance. Which shows how wrong even friendly officials can be.

After the interview we went for a medical examination. There was nothing inquisitive or malicious about this. Just a kindly need to be assured that we would live long enough to get our hands on part of the grant. The doctor looked at me briefly. I had had a year of intensive reading, using all available libraries and continuing my personal tradition of working in light so poor other people would not have been able to find the shelves. I had also been, when away from home, short of food, taking in less per day than many a caged bird. I must have looked frayed.

The doctor said I should not have as much to do with women. This for me was a new page in the script. I had, at that point, not even kissed a girl. I had known bouts of verbal excitement with those dredgers of sex jokes in the Welfare Hall, but in terms of serious experience I was as virginal as the physicist Newton, whose only asensual thrill was to be struck by an apple in flight and that on the head when he was asleep. I left the doctor's house with a stronger personality and a higher respect for myself. I could see myself making a more potent appeal to women interested in the worse forms of worldliness. I felt like Sydney Carton but without any urge to self-sacrifice. In the train on the way home I arranged my face into what I thought more telling lines of debauchery, and fixed women with such an insane glare of desire I emptied three compartments and almost got myself put off the train twice.

*

In the last term of my second year at Oxford I left for the University of Madrid. A stay in the country of the language one studied was obligatory. Had it not been I would not have stirred. Travel has never drawn me. Had I been able to subsist behind one rock, inside one small patch of ferny hillside, I would have done so. Nomadry I have always thought of as one of the most harmful roots of the human malaise. Even now, after numerous forays abroad to do commentaries for television films, I feel no more tolerant. Whatever the interest or beauty of the foreign cities taken in, the effect has always been wiped out by the memory of those gruesome Customs sheds and the stony custodians of the nation's commerce and morals who man them. We get fewer lepers but more officials at frontiers and the balance of unpleasantness is maintained.

Next to death and pogroms one of the most fiendish indignities on earth is to proceed from end to end of the divided land of Germany. At the first East German frontier we were fooled about by a group of young officials who could not have been jumpier if they had been told that Hitler was loose. Weary of their incessant poking and probing I told them I had a confession to make. I had a drugged Welsh physicist in the false bottom of the car's boot. I was almost shot for my impertinence.

At the crossing point from West to East Berlin we were processed like a herd of Chicago swine. Bored young soldiers, lounging around in some of the most dismal sheds to litter Europe since the Black Death, stamped their way slowly through every document on one's person. They even stamped a copy of the Welsh national anthem I always carry around with me against the day when a knowledge of its words will be the only cultural badge worth a damn in my rapidly self-emancipating land.

That night I had supper in a restaurant on the Kurfursten-damm. The star turn was a gypsy fiddler, a man of middle age and utterly unconfident. His playing was atrocious. I was hurt by the thinness of the applause, the indifference of the diners as they tried to drown the music with the champing of the teeth. I was in a mood to favour and praise anyone in the world who was not carrying a gun or stamping documents. At the end of an item I began to clap furiously. I must have nudged the conscience of the room. People put their knives down and clapped as loudly as I. The violinist was startled. He bowed violently. The applause increased. He bowed twice again, his head getting nearer to the floor. He overdid it. He snapped something and his trousers came down. A gale of mad laughter hit the place. The fiddler and I made up a small nucleus of chastened silence.

Latterly returning from New York I brought back a small gift of jade for my wife. I showed the jade but could not produce a bill. Officials conferred. I was marched off to a small room. I was submitted to a search similar in length and depth to those made on diamond-miners in the Rand, who, I am told, exploit every cranny of the human frame to secrete contraband. Even my personal notebooks, caught up, I suppose, in the Fanny Hill syndrome then sweeping the minds of our Chief Constables and the parlours of the pure, were peered at.

My handwriting, illegible to everyone except my wife, was regarded with suspicion. Such writing, they said, must be hiding something. I explained that it was even hidden from me because I couldn't read it either. They gave up eventually. I was mentally composing a telegram of ringing protest I planned to send to my Member of Parliament when a point of curiosity occurred to me.

'Tell me,' I said, 'do I look like the sort of chap who would really smuggle jade?'

'Frankly,' said the official, 'yes.'

I left that shed, as I left that doctor's house in Harley Street in the summer of 1932, a bigger, stronger man. To be attributed a gift that has never visited any corner of one's life is to know for a moment or two a new juice of identity.

That sort of problem did not arise on my first journey to Spain in 1933. Jade was the last thing I would have to declare. The officials would not need to confront me on that score. True, through smoking too much my face could sometimes take on a jade-like tint, but unless they were looking for a lump of jade shaped like a walking neurotic philologist they were not likely to bother me. Their glances, as I shuffled past their counters in the Customs shed at Dover, gave me to know that they did not expect me to cool the air in Europe, then poised for another fine new round of graveyards. (Hitler had been in the Berlin Chancellery honing his batch of lunacies for all of two months, and it was clear from the look of mental death in the eyes of our own government and all governments around that the morlocks were edging their way up the cellar steps.)

My companion on the journey was a sharp Yorkshireman who belonged to the same year and college as myself. His views and expression were loudly radical and pleasing to me. His father was a maimed veteran of the first world war and did something connected with the Haig Poppy Fund, an enterprise that tried to take the curse off Passchendaele and the Somme. My friend was later to become an eminent Civil Servant and even then showed signs of economic mastery.

When we met at Victoria station he was wearing a cloth cap. I had never seen him with any kind of head covering before and I showed my surprise. He gave no explanation beyond a wink. I felt it must be that he wanted to show the people abroad that he was not the usual kind of bullying imperial Briton.

We left Victoria on the midnight train. We spent the hours of waiting in a cinema. The film was *I am a Fugitive from a Chain Gang*. The price of admission was three-and-six. I had never paid more than a shilling before to get into a cinema. I was determined to drain the whole occasion of delight. I stroked the seat and smelled the ushers. There was a turn on the stage. A girl naked except for a few clusters of beads. She sang 'Chloe' and did a dance which consisted in the main of a contortion that used to be called Chinese Bend and the beads around the equator were dramatically stretched. A male dancer appeared from time to time and flung his arms around her thighs, sobbing his desire into the small of her back or her lap, and from where I sat his sobs were in order. If I had not been chilled by the price of the ticket I would have been up there with him. It was a great novelty.

Back home, ancillary turns in the cinema were rare. One cinema in Cardiff, a Babylonian place visited specifically as a treat, had an organist who rose from the basement to a height of about ten feet above the heads of the front row, riding his organ and playing as he rose. In the valley we would sometimes have reciters, failed actors who contributed to the theme of the film being shown. If the film were *The Shooting of Dan MacGrew* the reciter would speak a poem about MacGrew and at the poem's end would lurch from one end of the stage to the other, then fall flat to show that MacGrew had taken the bullet. But girls wearing only an ounce of beads and moving their bodies in ways that breathed soft bordello notes with every ripple, we never got as far as that, and even when we had a film about Salome the reciter stayed fully clothed.

About the film we saw, we saw it again in a cinema in the Puerta del Sol in Madrid for fourpence. It was half an hour longer, scenes of gross brutality in the Mississippi prison camp having been cut by the British censor. No Cora Pearl on the stage but the seat was soft and the air smokeless.

As we pulled out of Paris we were alone in the compartment. My friend took from his case a box full of sewing equipment, needles, thread, thimble, scissors, a complete outfit. My first guess was that he was going to sew a handkerchief to the back of his cap to protect the nape of his neck from the strong Spanish sun in the style of a Foreign Legionary. He took off his cap. He snipped open one of the cap's seams. He took out his wallet and removed some money.

'A third exactly,' he said, and I would never have said that one day I would sit within inches of anyone looking so shrewd. He stuffed the money into the cap. He was too absorbed to notice a man who paused in the corridor to admire his work. He sewed the cap back into shape.

He said, 'No sleep for me until we reach Madrid. You can take chances with your money if you like. Not me. My old dad has told me more than one tale about what a light-fingered lot they are once you pass Dieppe.' And he sat there primly, wide-eyed under his crown of sterling. Somewhere around Bordeaux, our sleepless night on the Channel steamer and the tension of the sewing caught up with him. He dozed off. I went to the water-closet. When he woke his cap was gone and he never saw it again. He never ceased to chide me for having, like St Peter, failed in a vital act of custodianship. I promised him that on the way back I would stuff money into my cap, catch a train that had the same prowler aboard and somehow even the account.

We reported at the University of Madrid to begin our studies. In those days the University stood on the city's very edge. Beyond it was ten miles of rough plain, then high sierra. From our lodging in the Carrera de San Jerónimo, a mere shout away from the Puerta del Sol, we reached the University in the most abominably congested tramcars. If you were going blue and actively choking when the conductor reached you, you travelled half-price with the promise of a rebate if you didn't make it alive to the terminus.

The University City was only half finished. It was the first secular University in Spain, built by the Republic set up in 1931 and furnished out of the few shillings left in the Treasury by the absconding Alfonso XIII. We spent a lot of our time with a hoarse, bland official called Sosa, who was always trying to get more money out of us. Every day a fresh exaction, a novel

University levy. Sosa plainly saw Higher Education as a new Charter for Chisellers. As my friend said, 'There's something of Yorkshire in you, Sosa.'

He had assigned us to a course for foreigners. The standard of Spanish in this course was elementary. We seemed to be listening through the shawl. The other people attending the course were all English, sharp-voiced and brimming with Saxon vim. They had been poured from a single mould and sounded as if they had all come from the same house in Tunbridge Wells. When they all spoke together, listening Spaniards would spin around as if struck again by Drake.

Nothing about the University seemed finished or ever likely to be. Haste and inadequacy could have furnished its motto. The lifts stuck so often they posted a resident lecturer in each lift to ensure continuity of teaching. There was a chronic shortage of money and Sosa tried to get it from us.

Three years after our arrival the dream embodied in the University took a fearful beating. It became one of the fronts in the siege of Madrid. Loyalists in the Faculty of Arts building, Moors and other Franquistas in the Faculty of Medicine, and in between villagers hanging out their washing and complaining about the behaviour of the visitors.

I took to slipping quietly away from my instruction. I would walk compulsively along the dusty plain towards the Guadarrama mountains, glittering still with winter snow. I had a wish to lose myself somewhere among those diamantine peaks. There was something not quite sane about the way I walked. I was in trouble with my body. My thyroid was over-acting to compensate for the lack of coherence on the academic front. I was producing gushers of thyroxine that brought me to within a drop of swilling me into the grave. When the toxins reached the top of the gauge my legs whipped into action and I kept walking until my mind started to spin and I flopped.

I never reached the Guadarrama mountains and after my statutory collapse with my thyroid steaming I returned to Madrid. There I was challenged by the Civil Guard, once struck by a wary villager and once charged by a bull. It was a fast bull. I ran until I felt my heart was going to burst all over Castille. I turned and shouted, 'For God's sake, listen.' I wanted to convey to the night, the bull, the world that between the malaise, my exile, my thyroid and the course for foreigners, I was not getting a good deal. The bull stopped, listened and turned back. I continued my walk to the University tram-stop, thanking the bull and feeling a bit like St Francis of Assisi.

I was smoking more than ever. Spanish cigarettes were twenty for fourpence and were called Canaries. They were rank and treacherous. They had a way of collapsing in mid-puff, burning ash dropping on your clothes, leaving just a fragment of paper dangling from your lips. They almost cured me of my stoop. If I smoked them with my back in its usual curve I usually managed to set my waistcoat ablaze. I smoked them by the thousand, sadly convinced that I was going to meet a strange end. I might as well choose to be incinerated in Spain. The Government monopoly and the smugglers who provided more tobacco than the monopoly urged the citizens to watch me and take a lesson from the gringo if they ever wanted to be able to lay on family allowances.

I withdrew without fuss from the course at the University. I used a small crypt in the city centre called the Philological Centre, stuffed with the most ancient fragments of Spanish writing. There I struck some of the worst light for reading even I had known, and if the folks at home could have raised the postage I would have gone daily into the crypt with a collier's lamp in my hat. Between the murk and concentration on acres of medieval missals I got back to the pension by touch.

The pension was cheap, ornate, full of Moorish doorways and uncommon plumbing. When we unplugged the bath the water flowed into the bath of the man next door. When he did the same we played reservoir for him. This tidal system took a few days to sort itself out, and it slowed cleanliness down to a hint. A source of emotional excitement in the place was the toilet. The seat was about ten feet from the door, and the hanging place for the roll loosely chosen.

One of the patrons was an old man with a grave cardiac

weakness. Time and again, after making sure with some major bit of rattling that the door was safely locked, he would take his ease and then collapse *in situ*. The lock would either have to be picked or the door forced. When the manageress and her aides pleaded with him to leave the door unlocked he said that as a fastidious Castillian he would rather be dead than do such a thing. In despair the manageress removed the lock and he died the next day.

In the dining-room our fellow guests were thickly bourgeois. Conversationally, lunchtime, dinnertime, the pattern did not vary by a comma. From the soup right through to the fruit they cursed the Republic roundly.

I withdrew again without fuss and with one eye still recognising things from the Philological Centre, not an inch added to my wisdom or joy. I took to long sessions of reading in the boulevard cafés. I bought cheap Tanchnitz editions of English and American novelists and poets. In the course of one enchanted day I read Thornton Wilder's *The Bridge of San Luis Rey* twice and Shelley's *Prometheus Unbound* once, both good statements on bad luck.

I did not stir. For food my body made do with three cups of coffee for one of which I was not charged by the waiter, a tall, loping Socialist utopian. My concentration was almost total. I looked up only occasionally to study the señoritos, the young Forsytes of Madrid, sitting languidly at their tables, impregnating lumps of sugar in brandy, then chewing them. I noticed that every time they opened their mouths the track of their caries had visibly broadened.

I became friendly with a man from the American Middle West. I never got to understand what his connection with Spain was, but he could not accept the place or the people. Everything in Europe he saw as underlining the American urge to move West. He would point to the most ill-assorted types, a girl in white for her confirmation or some other phase of loyalty to the Church, a uniformed beadle calming noisy worshippers outside a cathedral, the trumpeter in a brass band on its way to a bullfight who made no attempt to keep in line, step or tune with his fellows, and his comment would always be the same. 'Some kind of moron, I guess.' He felt, after a lifetime's exposure to the brisk sanity of St Paul, Minnesota, that Spain had long since slipped into a yawning cellar of imbecility.

But even from the boulevards I withdrew. I followed some kind of crypto-monastic urge that has flavoured a lot of my days. There is a lack of balance in my moral metabolism. I have only to take a peck at any single experience and I begin to fall back. My life must have been preceded by a sullen unwillingness to be born. I have a feeling that when my mother's time came to die she was full of serious doubts about the rightness or the decency of the genetic process. And she lived long enough to set me on the road to spread that message.

I retreated to my room in the pension. All around me were Spaniards and Spain and I had no real wish to know. My reading reached a peak. The whole of Shakespeare in the original, washed down by the translations of Menéndez y Pelayo. I ploughed a long deep furrow through the basic texts of world religion. This had always fascinated me and the quietness of being immured in an alien city gave my mind an edge of incomparable appetite. I was driven on by a feeling that I had not got the theological signal whole.

My Sunday School teachers had not been men who articulated boldly and the denomination to which they belonged had been riddled with doubt and diffidence, making them the shakiest sector on the whole theological front. The chapel in which they taught, never good acoustically, had been so affected by subsidence that odd sound pockets had been made in the twisted walls. One kept hearing sermons that had been made two years before and they had not gained in lucidity.

This told heavily against traditional beliefs and in favour of Frank Lloyd Wright, who had designed buildings which not merely smiled at ordinary subsidence but smiled serenely out of harm even in the teeth of mature earthquakes. So I wanted to check on things I might not have heard or misheard.

I read right through the Talmud, the two Testaments, the Koran and the Vedas and this intake, coupled with the plumbing and a deepening aggraphobia, made the going rough. So I wanted to get at the landscape of serene conviction, if such a place were accessible to me. All it did was aggravate a congenital urge to prophesy linked with an equally strong impulse to shut up because the news was always bad.

I also took in the output of Cervantes, Benito Galdos, Dickens, Dostoevsky, Tolstoy in interminable toto. I did the daily trip from Sinai to the sewers. I read a complete set of Marx and Nietzsche in Spanish and not a bit more toothsome for that. As a kind of Vichy water to swill that feast down I ran through about twenty paper-backed volumes also in Spanish of stories about Buffalo Bill Cody, 'shooter of bison, friend of distressed maidens and scourge of the Sioux'. That's what it said on one of the covers and by that time I was in a way to believe anything.

The only time I left the pension was when I was driven mad by indigestion and felt compelled to take a little exercise. I would walk from the pension front door and proceed about fifty yards along the kerb. Then I would pause, listen to the tumult of the Puerta del Sol, a noisy nerve of a place, a sort of Piccadilly with waves of unnatural laughter tagged on, and I would swiftly beat a terrified retreat back to solitude and the words.

Gastrically I stood on the Jordan. Tobacco, immobility and some strong brands of masochism had headed my stomach towards the valley of the elephants, and everything I ate tasted of old tusk. The rich oils in the food landed me with types of flatulence which, given time and space, would have unbalanced the weather.

Again and again I would be walking through a gay throng of Madrilians. I looked vindictive and cast a lot of gloom. Then a bit of distress would catch me and bend me double. The Spaniards would stop and bow back. It was a pleasant tableau.

In our rooms I would sing or hum a lot. My style of singing owed much to Bing Crosby, a sweet, honey-thick sound that tended to cling to the walls. This got on the nerves of my Yorkshire friend whose own singing was slight and toneless. A few bent bars from the *Messiah* and no more. He believed that anyone as prone to the singing of sentimental songs as I must be corrupt. He was either quite right or just jealous. Thirty years later I might have made the charts.

Once, while singing, I found the chambermaid at the door. She asked me, with great emotion, to repeat the song. The next day I found the manageress at the door. She told me, with great emotion, to cut it out or she'd call the police. The boom of my tone and my way of switching the note up or down an octave to suggest mastery and promote moral confusion had, apparently, been causing distress to the old man with heart trouble.

My singing covered a wide range, for despair, primed by my thyroid, invested my moods with an acrobatic variety. I was strong on some of the more violent recitatives from oratorio. First among these, and I think it was this one that brought the manageress to our door and drove my friend into the arms of Malaga wine, was 'Hear Me, Ye Winds and Waves' from *Scipio*. This shows Scipio, a failure and utterly fallen, sitting on a seashore and urging the gods to finish him off. I gave every note value.

In a softer key my favourite was a cut-rate American dirge called 'I'm Alone Because I Love You'. The pattern of notes suited my sombre style of delivery right down to the autumn ground, and the lyric hit off to perfection the mossy hopelessness of my mood. There was one couplet that cut my friend to the quick. 'Yesterday's sunshine has turned into rain. Yesterday's kisses are bringing me pain' 'Syphilis?' he would ask. Now and then, on hotter nights, I would stand on the small balcony and sing this song right down into the teeming Carrera de San Jerónimo. This did nothing to help the shaken Republic.

My friend and I did not travel home together. I never knew what other things he might have stitched into his cap on future journeys. He travelled south to Granada and nearly died of dysentery in the shadow of the Alhambra. I had had an idea that his rather chill temperament would react in some effusive way to the romanticism of that incredible anthology of gentle lusts.

My own journey home would have strained a Viking. The train was slow, because anything going at speed in Spain in those days provoked a crisis of displeasure among those people who saw an everlasting inertia as the best bet for the peninsula. The train was packed. Cows came in to inspect our tickets. Sitting opposite me were a peasant couple and their two children. They were eating a sandwich made up of an immensely long roll which had been hollowed, then stuffed with sausage, tomato and anything that happened to be handy. The loaf must have been five feet long. They did not break it or cut it. They just held it to their mouths and ate it.

They invited me to join them and made it plain that they would be slighted if I refused. I joined in and the five of us sat there for all the world as if we were blowing into a monstrous oboe.

I found a travelling companion, a massive Californian who had fled the murrain of the anti-saloon League in America and spent several years in Barcelona drinking good Scotch at abysmal prices. He had wandered in from his first-class compartment looking for conversation and a point of departure into drinking. Between incipient cirrhosis and a natural gift for depression he was a pessimist. He said that when Prohibition was removed America would find something equally lunatic to take its place.

'The impulse to risk and adventure is implicit in my people, and a capacity for madness is the most essential adjunct of that impulse. God help America when she has no more Wests to trample. The alcoholic Custer is our twin dream and nightmare. He is mixed up in most of our drinking, most of our weeping. Those bugles around the Little Big Horn were the most significant music we have ever made. We are always galloping at dawn out of some goddamned fort We have a great distaste for sitting still and looking at ourselves. We shall live out this century in a rising tide of drink, religion and violence. When I was in Barcelona and got very drunk I'd go and see a Western, praying for Custer and denouncing the nations of the Western Plains. A unique combination of goodness and madness, the Americans. Never trust any mixture of which conscious goodness forms a part. You're safer with madness.' And he would unwrap a couple of little glasses from a tissue and pour us a tot apiece.

As we approached the Basque country grave news filtered in from the platforms of the stations at which we stopped. It had rained in that region for forty days and forty nights. It was still raining with a ferocity that suggested that the rain had just heard of erosion and wanted to get on with it. There was an expression of Biblical doom on the faces we saw through the windows of the train. The mountains all around were on the move. There were more landslides than wheels on the permanent way.

At one station there was a man leaning on a handcart and laughing his head off. Between his laughter, his demented head-shaking and his way of splitting his every sentence equally into Spanish and Basque, he was hard to follow. A passenger explained to us that the man was a Basque nationalist and when the interest of that flagged he doubled as a religious maniac. He had been warning Spain for years of the approach of a cataclysmic flood. Now it was on its way. He was delighted. He looked forward to the moment when the Madrid government, the tyranny of Castille and our train vanished under the waters.

He asked the station-master if it was possible, now that a slight degree of autonomy was being granted to the Basque regions, for him to get the forms on which to apply for a subsidised ark. He was led off by two Civil Guards, who prodded him with their weapons and reminded him of the clause in the Constitution which forbade people to talk about rain in terms which might sadden the citizens. The man's laughter ceased.

'It'll be one of the gats that did that,' said the Californian. 'Not that crap about the Constitution. Always the gat.'

He sounded bland, his mind wrapped around a gallstone insolubly hard, as if he saw the future laid down a road of broadening darkness, broken by spasms of light from people and cities burning.

The peasant who had called me in as fifth man on that organ-pipe of a sandwich, a gentle, observant man, had one arm protecting both his children. They, full of bread and forcemeat,

F

were fast asleep. The man kept looking from the Californian, chuckling into his flask at the unchanging bloodiness of man, to the rain pelting outside, and his face suggested that the mind which links God and man was showing clear signs of weariness in the centre.

At the next station, Tolosa, a half-made place between vast hills, we were told there would be a long stop. The underpinnings of the track between there and the frontier had collapsed in several places. The station-master gave us a rundown on the situation. Labour gangs, comparable in size with those squads who had put up the pyramids, and mustered with a speed and from an area unique in the annals of the region, were slaving away at shoring up the sagging lines.

The Californian and I went into the station bar. His Spanish was simple. 'Un glasso de whisky, doble, y un sandwich de ham.' The bartender looked as if his language had been hit by subsidence too. As we came out of the canteen we saw our train moving backwards towards the South. We told a porter that our bags were on it. 'Señores,' he said, and he gave a bow that jerked his over-sized cap off. Normally there would not have been much to bow about in Tolosa. 'Señores, have no fear. It is a manœuvre, nothing more, nothing more.' Several times he turned away then came back saying, 'Nothing more.' He gave the phrase 'Nada más' sonority and force. He made it sound like a lament for life and Tolosa crossed with a programme for himself. He was obviously as fascinated by the word 'nada' as Hemingway. 'Nothing more.' He sounded as if he had been to the same night school as Poe and the raven.

Reassured, we watched the train vanish round a bend. We did not see it again for twenty-four hours. The Californian was convinced it was all part of some complicated heist. 'They undermine the railway, then head south backwards with the loot. We'll be here for ever. Wouldn't surprise me if that "nothing more" guy hasn't cut the wires in and out of the place.' We went back into the bar. By the time we left the barman was talking the same kind of Spanish as the Californian. Now and then the Californian would approach the porter. 'How many trains have you caused to vanish this month, Pablo? You're a magician, James.' (He would vary the name. James, Dalton, Tracy, all desperadoes of the American West.) 'What's the annual take, Pablo?'

When the train came back we were to wish that the manœuvre had gone on a bit longer. The train moved slowly out of Tolosa and did not pick up speed. Every time we got to a stretch of track where there had been collapse and repair we were told to leave the train, take our bags with us and walk, to lighten the load on the new and fragile substructure. This we did about eight times. The surfaces on which we walked were made of loose chippings. Chippings have never been more mobile. Twice they slid from beneath me and sent me shooting under the rail.

I would have landed up at the bottom of a Basque ravine had my descent not been checked by my bags or my coat been grasped by the Californian. My bags were heavy, my arms in agony and I wondered at what point of the elfin journey my load had switched from clothes and books to brass cauldrons.

The chippings were also large and sharp. The shoes I wore were light and cheap, and the chippings came slicing through the soles. I could feel my feet being unmercifully hurt. I was bent double with remarkable colours of anguish on my face. The Californian was equally beat. In his two huge cases he was probably carrying twenty bottles of Spanish Scotch and a bijou distillery. We were both fairly vocal, he denouncing the antisaloon League that had originally driven him from the States: I expressing the belief that my long reading in theology in the Madrid pension, coupled with my lacerated feet, might well make me the centrepiece of some new cult.

I said goodbye to the Californian at Irun. He said he would need three days of drink and sleep before he could tackle the next leg of his journey. I did not linger. I whipped through France like a breeze and attracted a glance or two as I did so. Between raging homesickness and chipped feet my mood was hooded. Those stretches of portage in the Basque mountains had done something to my arms.

It was beyond me to sling my cases on to the luggage rack and I sat hunched over them, giving the impression that I did not trust my fellow passengers. This created a nuisance. People tripped over the bags and my whole posture made a bad impression. I tried to win a bit of sympathy by stroking my shoes and groaning from time to time and repeating in slow fair French that in the Basque country it had rained for forty days and forty nights. I told them that as soon as I had come down from Ararat I had joined the people of Israel in their forty-year wait through the desert. I pointed at my feet and said that I had been tortured by the Inquisition for smuggling copies of Foxe's *Book of Martyrs* and Henry Miller over the Pyrenees. One of my fellow passengers said that the English would be backing a loser if they let me back in.

Every time I said that brought on a round of anti-British banter. I heard one person remark that he was glad to see an English eccentric with marks of poverty on him. It might mean that the breed were running out of funds and would now be obliged to stay at home and stop boring the French to death. By the time the train got halfway up France I had emptied the compartment. But even in solitude I did not have the heart to bare my feet and assess the damage.

I did some fine shuffling into the Gare du Nord, moving more slowly than a man making heavy weather of his ninetieth birthday. Even without my limp and stoop my appearance was now crumpled beyond belief. People looked at me with some curiosity, as if I might be a presage of the great hosts of refugees who would, within the next decade, be clogging and cursing the roads of Europe.

I did not pause on the way to London. I did not have the money to pause. On the Channel steamer I was famished. I hung around the dining-room dreaming of feasts and feeling as deformed and resentful as Quasimodo, denied a last bell-rope to swing from, a last breast to cry on. The money I had left would be just enough to cover the odd train and bus for the last lap of the journey inside Britain, and for a few cigarettes to damp down the flaring hints of famine. I asked a steward the way to

the bar. I wanted to see how far a bottle of lemonade and a bag
of crisps would take me towards fullness. He misdirected me
to some cavernous lazaretto where people were being seasick. I
gave in and joined them and saved sixpence.

That was the sixpence I squandered at Paddington station. I
decided to have a bath. The decision made me feel daring. Com-
ing from a home without a bathroom and shy about every aspect
of nakedness, my ablutions had always been furtive. Even when
sea-bathing in the course of Sunday School outings to the sea,
we had advanced down the shore with our hands scrupulously
shielding the crotch. I had certainly never experienced the
Moorish novelty of a public wash-house. But I felt some gesture
was due at Paddington. I was carrying half the dust of Castille
and Biscay on my person. My feet felt as if they had been set up
for a long round of bayonet practice. Besides I thought the fact
of being alongside the railway track that linked me at last with
the Western hills where I belonged merited some bit of cele-
brating. Getting clean from head to foot seemed a good way to
do it.

A sympathetic porter, seeing me totter towards the entrance
of the bath house, misinterpreted my state and asked me if I
had come up to London by hunger-march. At that period the
roads between London and the provinces were thronged with
vast processions of unemployed men protesting against their
idleness and poverty. They bore banners on which were written
axioms about economic justice taken from thinkers as far apart
as Jesus Christ and John Maynard Keynes. They wished to argue
the Government into the ways of a warmer humanity.

History has never recorded a more wanton waste of rage and
stamina. The Government, English sportsmen almost to a man,
were on a wicket of unique obtuseness and were in no mood to
be dislodged. When a Government has practised its hand over
years of small betrayals it is too much to expect them not to
move on to some massive sell-out of peace and sanity. Every
man has the right to work to get his name in heavier print on
the textbooks, even if it means making dead or humiliated mon-
keys out of half the species. The mission of the protesting

marchers was as futile as the winds their banners flapped in.
The insularity of their governors, in terms of human response,
had become, like so many of their better banks, marmoreal.

The sympathetic porter did not like the marches and he told
me I would have been wiser to stay at home. That way I would
not now be a sad and crippled supernumary at Paddington. He
saw the marches as a threat to himself. If more and more people
were going to move from place to place not on wheels but in
processions, this could be a knock to the railway trade. He
agreed with the protesters that the Government were a lot of
sods but they were established sods, proud of it, good at it, and
not to be messed about with. If you wanted to express dissent,
do it at home in a mutter. Silence was the only way. If I worked
at Paddington I'd see the point. He'd seen too many blokes
shopped by their own big mouths. He wanted to know what size
of banner I had carried on the march and what message had
been written on it. He said he liked reading.

'I am not a marcher,' I said. 'I carried no banner. I walk like
this because that is the way I feel about life, partly because some-
where south of the Pyrenees I lugged my cases over miles of
loose chippings. If you come into the bath-house with me I
will show you my stigmata.'

He turned away, and the hunch of his shoulders hinted that
with riddles being added to agitation the outlook was poor.

The bathroom attendant was glad to see me. Things in the
cleanliness line were slack and he added something about godli-
ness which I did not wholly catch. He gave me three times the
length of towel I would need. It took me at least thirty dolorous
minutes to get my socks away from my feet. The raw flesh had
knotted itself into the wool. I felt like a fakir out of luck whose
big nail trick has come unstuck.

I groaned a lot, a good baritone effort. It sounded fine in the
white-tiled chamber. I soaked myself for an hour. Every fifteen
minutes the attendant would knock on the door and ask if I was
all right.

'I thought you might have drowned or fainted. It's the deep
bath. Most people are used to very shallow articles. I've seen

people go in there two or three feet too short for the length of the bath. They panic and they wait for me to get the Fire Brigade to winch them out. And a lot of them come from places where the smells are gloomy, and the fine, scenty soap we use here comes as a big shock to them. Aggravates the sex element in some of them. Had to speak harshly to them to get the thing tamed. The warm water, the scenty soap and the strange unknown place. A bad mixture. Plays hell with the pure in heart who want value for their sixpence. Thought you looked a bit rough when you came in here. I thought what a terrible thing if you came all this way to end it all. These days you don't know what's going to crop up next. I wouldn't want any gloom to fall on my bath-house. A sad enough place already, Paddington. People meeting, passing, coming, going. Tides, tides. Like a stretch of seashore but less fresh.' He shook my hand. 'I am genuinely glad to see you coming out of there, safe and sound, because there was a funny look on you when I handed you the towels and explained to you the mysteries of the taps. And you smell a treat. And what's more, you've left the bath spotless. That's more than I can say for some of the rodneys who've rinsed themselves between these walls. By God, they've left the bath looking like a length of new road. But you, different. A new pin. I should keep you here to explain to the clients what should be done.'

I was glad to hear him say that. After my soak I had rinsed the bath of four or five pounds of dense, Peninsular dirt. I had been able to identify the various Spanish provinces in the layers of ochre waste.

I shook the attendant's hand and walked to my train feeling as light as a feather, clean, sockless, wise, more conscious of my own past and the future of Europe than ever before, and damnably depressed about both.

*

My terms at Oxford were from beginning to end a series of spinning alienations. At the end of my second year my friend

Wynne Roberts went down with a degree of low value, an evaluation that reflected absolutely nothing of his real talent, but that, I suppose, is the true function of degree giving. Intelligence of the more passionate kind is its own joy and fulfilment. Its assessment by people smugly dull enough to be assessors is hardly ever relevant.

I mean here no flattery to the failed, no unfairness to the adjudicators. I suggest only that competition in any context under the sun is a bloody farce. Competition in the world of higher scholarship, of fine perception, is something worse. The judgments struggling to emerge in the mind of a late adolescent are hardly ever capable of being judged. There is too much blood and pain and witless arrogance on them.

Everything in education tends to be about ten years before its proper time. The 11-plus should be the 21-plus. The degree examination should be the 31-plus. Parturition should be vastly prolonged if only to curb the manias of the philogenetic, and death made subject to a County Council vote. All the same the tendency of dolts to proliferate and rule in our academic life is probably a blessing. Without the bellowing of the stupid, the brighter side, the more nakedly perceptive flanks of our existence would probably be an unbearable nuisance. The morons carry the Shelleys in quick and justifiable coffins to the grave.

At least I can say that when Wynne Roberts died, many years after his bad and deplorably misleading graduation, to my senses the level of pain in this world was sensibly lowered. He never really forgave his judges. Nor should he have. Nor should they yield in their judgment of him. Vagrant bits of genius, and that boy was festooned with them, should be accorded no more worth than the vagrant bits of waste that float on the water-surface of sewers. Disinfection is in. Creative pity is out. And Wynne, with his promiscuous passion, would have agreed.

I will never cease to be grateful to him, utterly different from him as I was, for I was in every regard so other from what I would have wished to be. I was clumsy at kindness, gifted at turning away, cursed with an imperfect sense of community, while denying myself the gains that these ghastly qualities might have brought me in. I am one of the great legion of bastards who have never really paid off, lacking just the bit of greed and callousness that might have put teeth in my resentment. And that probably reflects some diet deficiency. A sort of moral rickets, a terror of being richly vicious. I am glad, for the vile, however gently, must be curbed. But I would have wished a knowledge of Wynne on all mankind, for through himself he conveyed the whole experience of all those peculiar, lovely people who by their words or attitudes have caused some new flower to bloom in our wilderness, some new hint of resurgence in our long, drowned shame. He set so many thoughts alight the Philistines complained against the lessening of their favourite child, the dark. His only reaction was to ask how the rates and taxes were in Philistia, for he was against exactions proposed from above. He was destroyed by too many brands of wisdom in a world unripe even for the absorption of one brand of sapience.

Wynne's generosity had the fluency of water, the flavour of wine. If a kindly uncle chanced to drop by and slipped him ten pounds, four of the pounds passed invariably to me, for all the world as if I were operating some kind of protection racket. The response from me was nil. The uncles I had were not kindly and would have passed through Oxford only as members of one of those protest marches. Besides I never sufficiently believed in money to dish it out. Wynne had various types of social skill and confidence that never came my way. He was useful with a telephone and walked in and out of banks with real elation. And there was this zest for gift-making, probably the most dynamic of all social arts.

For myself, Edison could have stuck to quoits. If I wished to communicate with people at a distance I favoured drums, pigeons or a quick shout. As for banks my link with them was sub-Eskimoid. In the matter of making gifts a hand would need to be paralysed or dead to work more slowly than mine. Any relationship that needs to be fed with gifts strikes me as being an impudent freak. My life is so full of unacknowledged birthdays and other anniversaries there is a feeling among many of my kin that life must have ground to a stop.

I can recall only one act of altruism performed by myself towards Wynne. It followed some stupidly childish outburst by me, probably in answer to the smell of his pipe or the manhandling of his large gramophone from the bus stop to our lodgings. I went down into the town and prowled up and down the High Street resolved to sweeten the air and my own name with a bit of propitiation. I bought a one-pound tin of John Cotton tobacco, of which I had heard Wynne speak highly. I also managed to lay my hands on a second-hand disc of the slow movement from Mozart's clarinet concerto in A major.

Wynne was delighted. He was not merely glad to receive the gifts in themselves. He was astonished to see me practise the normal banalities of graciousness. There was a touch of frenzy in his gratitude. To make his delight utterly plain he smoked his way right through the tin of John Cotton without pausing to eat. He played the Mozart record on the same non-stop basis, deepening the ruts in the record's fabric to a point where you could virtually hear both sides at once. Given time he would have had it looking like a doyley. He suffered for both bits of excess. The smoking drove a long-standing cough into a whooping fury that had us banned from two cinemas. The record put him off clarinets for life.

The vacations were sweet. Each term's end seemed to bring a drift of sanity back into my days. Few things remain in my mind of the whole experience. It is strange that for so many men Oxford remains a sanctified stretch of golden road, a totem pole of fulfilment to be showered with the kisses of a tireless affection. I envy them. It's good to have behind one one piece of rounded satisfaction, laughing times. But dredge as I will I can find in my hand only a few dried fragments. Being hurtled into the river by some manic coach on a bicycle: listening at a Balliol concert to a chorus of crickets going all out in the college kitchen and coming within a click of drowning a Beethoven sonata: startling a roomful of examiners when I fainted from pure fatigue halfway through the last paper of my final examination: copying out hundreds of extracts from prescribed texts, pinning them to the walls for easier viewing until the room was literally a catacomb of quotations: receiving tins full of Welsh cakes from my sister Nana and having a younger undergraduate than I saunter in each evening and take one without saying a word: hearing the bell of the college chapel tell my mastoid bone that it had singled me out for special treatment from the start: solitude tainted from top to bottom with the taste and smell of digestive biscuits, meat pies and cocoa.

But the hills around the valley brought solace. My thyroxine was at high tide and I paced the hill-tops daily to keep the toxins tame. There was a good deal of night walking too. It started as a solo effort by myself, brought on by the insomnia that had come from excessive cerebration, the riot in my glands and an unwillingness to have sleep cheat me of an extra cigarette, but on nights of ample moonlight I was joined by some of my brothers and friends, and we struck the note of a happy coven as we walked through the shadows over the ridge that lay to the south of the village, over the beautifully shaped moorland and down into the Vale of Glamorgan, a curiously idyllic place in contrast with the exposed vein of industry, wealth, squalor and absurd aberration which the Rhondda had become.

The place we headed for was a township called Llantrisant which clings to a hill in the manner of Toledo, but less dogmatically. It was there that a doctor called William Price, a man against whom my mind keeps jumping, slipped cremation into the social curriculum and nearly got himself lynched for his pains. I've mentioned this before, boastfully, for our area has not been rich in novelty.

His life was quick, varied and incredible. As a young medical student he became a brilliant supporter of the Chartist radicals, who were urging the Duke of Wellington to stop thinking of life as an unfolding facet of death and grow up. Price was forced to flee the country with writs threatening a lifetime of gaol or a quick noose fanning his fugitive buttocks. He went to the Sorbonne and studied surgical midwifery.

His principal persecutor was a powerful and equally talented man called Crawshay, who supervised the making of iron in a place called Merthyr, and married a sullen artefact with an equally sullen place. There are still places in Wales that can darken the sun faster than Merthyr, but not many.

After Price's flight to France, as time passed and, with the shooting, hanging and gaoling of various dissidents less passionate about humanity after seeing so much of its basic works, tempers cooled. Price, a graduate and himself less partial, felt it was safe to return. The story of his return has a thick Hollywood stripe in it. He slipped ashore at Cardiff, not quite sure of what his reception would be. His old enemies were tough and unrelenting. He decided to lie low until he was sure that the gaolers and hangmen have crossed him off their list. In general terms he feels no resentment against the authors of his exile. One man only he feels he can never forgive.

An envoy of Crawshay seeks him out. Crawshay's wife is dying in child-bed. He had heard of Price's studies in surgical midwifery at the Sorbonne. He begs Price to help. Price helps. The lady survives. The tale is perhaps too pat to be plausible. But with Price the truth always walked around with a bizarre flourish.

There was always a nourishing solemnity in walking up the hill into the soundless town, thinking of Price and death and flames.

Odd things happened on those long rambles over the hills and under the moon. There was a wall on the high moorland against which we rested out of the wind at about half past two each night. We would always for a few seconds at a time feel the earth shake beneath us. This might have been the effect of exhaustion or some nervous reaction felt by day people to an excess of darkness. Or it might have been a genuine shake. Somewhere in one of Robert Louis Stevenson's travel books he describes how while crossing the Pyrenees he repeatedly at night, about two-thirty to three, had the feeling that the mountains had been taken up by a huge but pacific hand and rattled.

My father claimed that when he worked the night shift in the pits he had often, at about the same time, been aware of a great cosmic shudder. Just as if the world were shrugging its shoulder or expressing a wish to fill its man-made holes. The ponies he tended felt it too, for they would neigh in union and that racket did nothing to ease my father's terror. We listened to his evidence without much conviction. Above ground or below it he lived in a world that tended to spin and come adrift.

There was also a teacher at school whose mind was full of memories of the nights he had spent standing guard during the campaign of the Dardanelles. He would watch every movement of the moon and try to keep his mind off the darkness and the sound of Turks trying to slip a knife in before the dawn. He had often referred to this pre-dawn tremor. But we remembered that often, at all times of the day, we had seen this man stand still, his legs wide apart, bracing himself against some shock that was coming along to send him hurtling on to his back. Besides, in the task of taking the mind at night off things like Turks and knives any tactic of the imagination is licit.

Near Llantrisant was a slope called Smilog Hill. On the hilltop was a spring that gushed abundantly. Its water had a purging power of atomic scope. We lay flat on the damp, cool grass and drank deeply. We returned slowly home, our minds exalted and our insides shaken with terror and delight by the rinsing course of the mineral spring. Our bodies grew marvellously tired. Had the social code of the region not been slanted so severely against vagrancy we would have gone to sleep on the pavement.

Of the real countryside I have never known very much. I have been mixed up in various untidy expeditions into the fields, leading groups of schoolboys to help harvest crops of simple plants like potatoes, mangels, carrots. Much of this activity we found grotesque. The earth, without fail, was hard and the farmers uncharming when not hostile. Our labours served to load the plates of the population in time of war, and no man's life is less full for having enriched a few greengrocers. We might have buried a voter or two in excess starch but we caused no deaths:

The ambience of the countryside has always repulsed me. I have knocked but have never been admitted. Places where horses

and dogs are afforded a love and significance not given to
humans alarm me. A horse-ridden village appals me as much as
the greed-ridden centre of cities. From these two sets of places,
the subhumanly callous and the supernormally vile, I must, in
previous lives, have fled like a whippet. Atavistically, I would
bet, I have lived cheek by jowl with people in flight from des-
tructible cultures and threatened frontiers. Whenever I look
back into the past the air is suffused with smoke from my
smouldering and fugitive tail. I am a hare that will always run.

The first time I experienced the real deep countryside, the
area of earth and feeling that remains eternally alien to one who
has never penetrated the hedges, was during my first summer
vacation from Oxford. The invitation came from a boy whose
friend I had become during my last year at school. His name was
Norman and his father was in some part of the northern reaches
of the Welsh border. He had come to the valley to spend a year
under the headmastership of E.T. with whom he had some
family connection.

Norman was large, genial, helpful and very lazy. He had a
warm general interest in the world but his studies had not
flourished. It was thought that E.T., who by now had a reputa-
tion for inducing energy even among the less dedicated of the
dead, might send Norman off to a flying start. This did not come
about but it got me my invitation to the country.

Norman had given me no indication of what his parents did.
I had certainly never before heard the name of his native village.
He was to meet me at the nearest town and guide me in. I was
eager to go. After that first year at Oxford I felt disturbed, un-
balanced, and I wanted something that would soothe me back to
normal. I did not know that the sensation of falling off cliffs and
going headlong over stretched ropes in the dark was going to be
a fixed feature of my being. In any case, that village, as it turned
out, would not have qualified as a cure for anything very much.

I was curious to know what a village looked like, a genuine
village. The homeplace to which we gave the name was little
more than a smoking meteorite on and around which people
had been dragooned into living. There was nothing of the

bucolic about it. It was a place made in a hurry by men for the
enriching, entertainment and degradation of men.

I had been nourished in the early years of my French course
by a vast, coloured picture of a French farmyard. The teacher,
in a quick, droning voice, would ask us to pick out in French
the farmer, the pig, the cockerel, the pitchfork, the trough and so
on. The teacher was an indolent man whom this style of teach-
ing suited well. He had been around that farmyard so many
times there was nothing left in the picture that would have him
running around the room. He would have been interested only
if the farmer and his creatures started to sing, for he was an
ambitious precentor with an itchy baton. But we loved the pic-
ture. We had a vision of France as a plump, pacific place and
whenever I go to France to this day I tend to drift towards the
Ministry of Agriculture to find out how things, over the years,
have gone in that well-stocked yard which had, for us, except
in those moments when some unalert student identified the pig
as the pitchfork, the enchantment the frieze on the Grecian urn
had for Keats.

There were other reasons for wanting to visit Norman. I had
never been to stay with anyone before, never slept under the
roof of a friend and I regarded this as a social notch of some
importance. There was also an emotional impulse. After that
course of meat pies and digestive biscuits at the transport café off
Carfax at Oxford my libido had sharpened. I was trying with-
out any sure knowledge of the route to break into the ranks of
serious lovers. My target was a girl who lived in the town's
biggest house. Her father owned an abattoir and she had a
great collection of vivid tartan skirts on the short side, which
stood out like a sunrise in a place where the garments of women
tended to be long and dun.

The abattoir was shrinking. The local economists were con-
vinced that in all the world only a tiny privileged minority was
getting any meat. But his daughter's skirts were attracting a fine
audience. She was a well-trained flirt. She had dozens of the lads
dancing around her, and I was the most laggard, least confident
member of this band. She would lure the others, then call them

to halt with a tinkling laugh. For me she did not even tinkle. Whenever I managed to pronounce an audible word in her presence, and got my eyes close enough to hers to suggest ardour, she would bring me crashing down with a series of crushing rebuffs, sending me scurrying back to my philological belfry.

Imagine all the devices perfected by provocative women for keeping boys fruitlessly on the hop, this girl in the tartan skirts had gone through the catalogue. And I was the lamest hopper in her attendant team. So I looked forward to a fortnight of not having to moon around this enchantress. I saw Norman's village as a desert fort where I could skulk like an oblivious Legionary.

I took the cross-country bus to Worcester. Norman met me on the town square and we boarded a bus that looked as if it was on the last day of a life of shortening journeys. We made our way towards the village, through endless, lush July lanes. It was like sliding down a green well. Norman told me that the area, behind its apparent serenity, boasted the highest recorded number of convictions for bestiality—people having carnal traffic with animals.

This interested me. In the valley people spent so much time denying elbow room to sex, the elbows of the adventurous had taken on a sensitive life of their own. And here were people not content with the normal curriculum of postures and partners, but were adding byres and kennels to the conventional beat. I looked at the thick hedges with a fuller respect and peered more intently out of the bus windows to see if I could spot the beginnings of some scandalous joust. Norman told me to save my eyes. By day people worked mostly. Things did not perk up until after dark. As long as the sun shone passions did not become sinister.

The farmhouse of Norman's parents was solid and a few centuries old. We arrived in time for what I took to be an early supper. It was a huge bowlful of hot milk loaded with bread and butter. We ate it on a bare table. The floor was flagstoned, the walls rough. Everything was anchored in work and time.

Every word spoken the silence seemed to resent. It had a curious effect on my ears, used to the ceaseless, crowded clatter of our kitchen at home, the shouting valley. It reminded me of the opening of any French novel about the wilder reaches of the countryside. A team of funny possibilities seemed to be lying in wait behind each leg of the table.

Norman's mother was sweet and compassionate. She fussed around me, urging me to spoon up my milk and bread at a faster speed. She clearly thought the shadow of urban disease hung as emphatically on me as my suit. But there was something in her eyes that did not match the placidity of the background. Norman's father was a brooding man who said hardly a word. He was out of Nathaniel Hawthorne and the journey had been hard. He alternately sighed and cooled his milk and there was no tonal difference that I could hear. He wore a big beard. It seemed not to belong to him. When he moved he seemed to be separated from it by a clear foot as if he could not bear to touch or think about the things that had prompted him to grow it. His life had been a constant pendulum from manuring to mourning and back.

The parents sat at the further end of the big table from myself. They spoke, but to one another, not to us. I could not hear what they were saying. The mother looked at me from time to time. The father looked down into his milk. Norman sat in silent embarrassment. The mother raised her voice slightly. 'We should tell him.' The father shook his head. 'No, you won't.' He looked grim. He finished his milk and went off to bed, although it was still quite light. He nodded his head at me but did not say good night.

Shortly afterwards Norman and his mother showed me to my bedroom and went to theirs. They clearly believed in knocking the day sharply over the head. I heard the whirring of an owl and some disturbance in the thatch. I bolted the bedroom door. I had never in my life done this before. I have always hated exclusiveness. I felt that strange blend of pride and shame which, in strictly chemical terms, probably explains leukaemia. I unbolted the door, inviting all the forces on earth, however

G

malign, to come flooding in. Then I heard a voice. It was not Norman's. It was not his father's nor his mother's. It was deeper, more commanding, and it rumbled through every wall of the house. I bolted the door again and tried to get in touch with the owl to get a bit of warmth back into the evening again.

I got into bed. When I awoke it was pitch dark. But it was not the coming of the full dark that had ended my sleep. A hand of enormous strength was beating on my door and tugging at the latch. And the owner of the hand was uttering messages in a voice of incredible power but not to be interpreted by anyone like myself.

I dived towards the window, opened it and found the owl there, sitting right on the ledge and grinning as if it had been returned with a vast majority. The voice of the man pounding at the door became more urgent. I wanted to leap through the window. The owl wouldn't budge. Given a blither background of romance I might have tried marrying it. But I was beyond help in that line.

The landing filled up with people. I could hear Norman's voice and his mother's, pleading. I could hear his father's voice, threatening. There were sounds of scuffling, of someone being pulled but not yielding much. There followed fifteen minutes of muttering, shuffling, shoving, groaning. Then there was silence. Even the owl left. I could not sleep. The night became tangible. I followed the breaking of the day, bit by bit, in sound. I had a vision of the day picking up the fragments of itself, blindly, grudgingly. Twice I felt like getting up and giving it a push. But there was no more pounding on the door.

At breakfast the following morning the pattern was the same as at supper. Norman's father and mother sat at one end of the table, he and I at the other. We had eggs; they were back on the warm milk and bread. Norman was uneasy and said nothing. The parents spoke in undertones and what they were saying was an exact echo of the night before. 'We should tell him.' 'No, you can't.' My thyroid was responding to the situation like a setter. It was telling me that if I didn't go home at once it would leave without me.

After breakfast Norman suggested a walk to the local grave-yard which had associations with a poet and a group of ancient, misshapen trees. I was all for it. After that shaking night I could do with trees and the company of the dead. I found I was without a handkerchief. I said I would nip upstairs and get one from my case.

The tensions had aggravated my stoop and I was bent nearly double as I began to climb the steep staircase. Halfway up, my head ran into some white fabric. One of my hands leaped forward in shock. It touched a foot. I looked up. In front of me, motionless as the wall, was a man of about twenty-one, one of the largest and most impressive-looking men I have ever seen. He was wearing a white nightshirt that came down to the ground and he had a black beard that covered his chest. His eyes were bright and beautiful and reason had departed from them long since. He put out his hand to touch me. I dropped back down the stairs, literally. My feet had nothing to do with it. I resumed my seat in the kitchen. I heard the man climb the stairs and close a door behind him. Norman and his parents looked hard at me. And still they said nothing.

I followed Norman to the graveyard. It seemed to be the only part of the village clearly in view. The trees were every bit as misshapen and ancient as Norman had said. Their roots were massive and vagrant and over the centuries had thrust up a host of bones. This had given a deep sense of insecurity to the village. Norman forgot to tell me about the poet with whom the graveyard had a link. I asked him about the bestiality for which the village held some kind of record.

He gave me some astonishing examples and for a few seconds my mind broke loose from that vision of the man on the stairs, and my thyroid crept back from the spot in the next county where it had landed in one terrified leap at the sight of those staring, stricken, dangerous eyes.

At lunch they told me the story. Norman's mother did most of the talking. His father asked to be excused long before she had finished and went back to his work, trembling with what might have been rage or embarrassment, leaving his food untouched. The man who had battered his fists on my door was the man I had seen on the stairs. He was Norman's brother, Sam. He was the second of three sons. The eldest was in Birmingham doing a job connected with milk. He never came home, having quarrelled with his father.

Sam had been unwell, said the mother, for six years. At the age of fifteen he was already large, powerful and passionate, each appetite in full bloom, capable of doing in every field the work of four men. He had fallen in love with the village trollop, a girl who had already enthralled and infected half the men in the area. The father's anger at this had been wild. He had kept his own passions caged and flogged, and he had no wish to see a son of his made a fool of by lust. He had threatened the girl with a whip and tried to beat the fever out of Sam. But the fever stayed, burned his body, bit his brain and daily through a blue May and June his father worked him to within an inch of torpor.

Then one blazing day in July the father was bending over some task or other in the fields. He heard a quiet footstep behind him and saw a shadow fall over him. He spun round and saw Sam standing over him swinging a scythe to behead. He flattened his body and felt the breath of the blade as he rolled out of danger. He sprang to his feet. Sam was off balance from the force of the swing. The father knocked him senseless with one blow, then slapped him awake.

Sam got up and ran to the house, screaming and weeping, as mad as a man can be. He went up to his bedroom and stayed there. Sometimes when some residue of curiosity stirred in his broken mind he would come halfway down the stairs, stand there for hours in his nightshirt like some grotesque prophet, but no further than that. His beard had grown and the father had grown one to reduce the air of strangeness.

The family doctor had pleaded with them to have Sam placed in care. The mother had given him a fanatical no and said that Sam would remain with her beneath that roof until the day he might choose to die. It was on this issue that the first son had quarrelled and left home. He had wanted to see the back of

Sam. They had seen the back of him instead, and now he was doing quite well with the milk in Birmingham. The mother said she was sorry she had not been able to give me the whole picture as soon as I arrived, but they had hoped Sam would remain quiet during my stay, and anyway it was difficult to explain things of this sort during a meal. I said that was all right. I said I thought Sam was a fine, handsome man, and I felt sure that one day he would be himself again and would come down to the kitchen, right as a rainbow, the storm exhausted. She smiled.

During the remaining days at the farm I could not shake off a sense of darkness. I spent a lot of time in the graveyard, listening to the ancient trees creaking towards some final act of decay, and creating unease among the bones. One evening Norman pointed out Sam's trollop to me. She had a crumpled face, was standing against a tree and was being roughly embraced by an elderly ploughman who kept looking over his shoulder as if he had been caught at this game too often already. She kept jerking his vagrant head back into alignment and there was a force about her face and fingers that made me understand how men, sharing her with a few other pitiless pressures, could be made to drift away from reason.

Nobody put up an argument when I suggested that I leave before the fortnight's end. Norman and his parents saw me on to the village bus. The father's mood had curdled since my arrival, as if the presence of a stranger had jerked apart the lips of ancient wounds. He had imposed some heavy field tasks on Norman. He had made it plain that he thought it would do me the world of good to join in. I had told him that my branch of the Celts belonged to the Beaker Folk and the closeness of arable land brought out all our weaknesses. He tried me out on a few simple tasks. In no time I proved to him that technically I still had my nose pressed hard against the further side of the Stone Age. The salvation of the world may one day come from a handful of people who feel that way. Unless we run out of stone as well, or my lot may decide that the world's salvation is work as unseemly and sinister as factory labour or the making of cities.

So I made the bus journey from the village to the county

town alone. Since that day I have not seen that farm, Norman
or his parents: nor have I heard anything about them. I like
leaving these points of darkness behind me and then, on odd
nights, to let the points glisten with curiosity, a private jewel-
case of flights, omissions and tiny betrayals.

I had a long wait for the coach on the main square of the
country town. I spent a minute or two looking at a cathedral,
but the sight of the solemn, robed officials who have their being
in such places robs them, for me, of all their possible beauty.
Churches are infested hillocks and I do not like their choice of
gnomes. While I waited a procession of clergymen, with vest-
ments as heavy and proud as the hand of their authority, passed
on some errand of observance or commemoration. I have never
been able to watch such spectacles without a sense of being
pleasantly baffled and utterly excluded. Pomp and dogma are
the two legs of our species, and the scamps and fools they have
kept in motion will not readily see them broken.

I was drawn to the entrance of the local Woolworth's. The
gramophone-record counter was near the door. The girl who
had the job of playing the records to advertise the stock was
small, sweetly sad and musically a monomaniac. She played just
two records incessantly. Both had tears making a bid for world
power and coming close. The first was Bing Crosby singing his
theme tune 'Where the Blue of the Night, Meets the Gold of
the Day', then penetrating Europe for the first time and making
the sour phobias of the epoch, for anyone with the least bit of a
baritone voice, more bearable. The second was a waltz called
'Auf Wiedersehen'.

This was to become very popular in the valley, but not under
its proper title. German, to our people, was a strange and un-
welcome tongue. 'Auf Wiedersehen' became, for the most
casual reasons you can imagine, 'To Peterston'. Peterston is a
village of supposedly romantic character in the vale which ad-
joins the valley and the new title fitted in quite well to the
lyric. But it puzzled some of the more analytical crooners of the
zone who had never before heard of Peterston.

The two songs had a big effect on the girl behind the counter.

She was crying overtly on to the wax of the records. Even from as far away as I stood, her tears could be seen glistening on the shiny black surface. The manager of the store, a short, barking man, came up and told her that this was a sure way of harming Woolworth's. He told her to dry the records with her handkerchief because salt played hell with the grooves. He selected a record that would bring romance to heel. It was a recording by a heavy contralto of 'Abide with Me', a slow and suffocating hymn associated with occasions of mass grief and remembrance.

My coach came in. I entered and waited for people and luggage to settle down. I opened my window and concentrated my ear on Woolworth's. I had some mental money staked on what was going to happen to that record. It happened. The contralto was cut off in mid-phrase. She was approaching that line about foiling the tempter's power when the needle rose and the record was changed. Bing Crosby was back on his twilight beat. I was glad. 'Abide with Me' is not a song that exalts me. To my ears it is most foully hooded by thoughts of wars and nationally significant football matches.

Besides, those two steamy melodies and pleading lyrics had touched my mood with softness. I briefly had a thought of the girl with the tartan skirts who lived in the town's largest house, and had the town's largest following of virgin and frustrated lovers. I dropped the thought. The immediate presence of Sam, his trollop as accessible as any docks, his father impaled on the prongs of a murderous moral joke, that, and a sense of the lost and festering loveliness beneath and behind every human habitation, had pushed me beyond the reach of any flippancy. I was putting the finishing touches to a trough of creative depression which was to be my fixed address for a fair number of years to come.

The sound and motion of the coach touched me like ether. My emotions were yawning and my body relaxed. I fell asleep humming, oddly, 'Abide with Me', casting a gloom over the man who was sharing the seat with me. It was his eyes that suggested sleep to me. I had a dream. It was a dream about Norman, his family, the farm. It was a dream that was to hang around the beds of my life like an unwanted dog. How does a tight, desperate situation like that end? Does madness establish a moat of other protective madnesses around itself? Does the compassion that ignores reason and prolongs anguish suddenly recognise its danger and clear itself like a storm-cloud out of the sky? These are the sort of questions best answered asleep in a bus. The dream opened with the face of Norman's mother staring at me across a lagoon of warm milk. She says: 'I remember you said that an owl landed on your window-sill that first night you were with us. I don't remember any owl doing that on one of our window-sills before. It must have been that that made Sam wonder about what things were moving about in the night. It was that brought Sam wandering to your door. Quiet as a mouse usually, Sam. But strangers and owls would make him uneasy.'

She vanishes. I see the years pass, labelled and in file, like convicts. Norman has left the farm, never to come back. One afternoon his parents go by car to the county town. On the way back the car stalls and is utterly destroyed by a train. It take a long time to decide who they are. The family doctor is informed. He remembers about Sam. He gets assistance and hurries to the farm. Sam is not there. The last flash of the dream shows Sam in a clump of trees. He is still in his nightshirt. He is staring at the windows of a brilliantly lighted house.

I have carried three such brutally recurrent dreams through my days and each one has been a damned nuisance, its teeth and lips fixed around my thoughts with vampirical authority leaving not even a muddy residue of calm. I plunge through the usual paraphernalia of unease: bogs, back lanes, mobile inquisitors, dumbness in moments meant for overmastering music or eloquence, landslips, whole landscapes caught up in a rumba of crumbling perfidies. Through this maze of lunatic and minatory images Sam moves like a transferable joker. At the end of each phase of squalid absurdity Sam stands in his clump of trees and his nightshirt, bereft, wondering, staring at those lighted windows. He starts singing 'Auf Wiedersehen' with overtones of 'Abide with Me'. I am standing by Sam's side, joining in, and embarrassed by his nightshirt and his inability to harmonise.

Then I switch to become a face behind one of the windows at which Sam is staring. Sam starts moving towards the house.

When I woke the man with whom I was sharing a seat in the coach was just managing to hang on. He told me that if he had to share a seat again with a sleeper as dynamic as I he'd be off buses for good. He asked the conductor of the coach to strap me down or put me off.

*

When I left Oxford I salvaged fifty pounds from my bijou finances. I did this by bits of chicanery so minute they cannot be described. I had a clear idea of what was to be done with the money. I would live at home, allowing myself a pound a week pocket-money, then I would die of natural causes. This thought caused me no misgivings. The world was full of marching maniacs and wounded economies. I was spent. The years of study with no relief of change or pleasure had burned my nerve-ends to ashes. I felt I had reached a point beyond the power of any miracle to revivify.

I approached my end with a kind of sinister jollity. I knew that, dying at twenty-two, I would regret not having travelled a little more, not having heard more music, not having made genuine love with willing women, but these things took second place to my desire to ease myself slyly and without fuss through the next door. I had never felt so masterful or wise.

It was a daft, hallucinated year. My excess thyroxine was in a state of fine ripple, washing away all the bridges that might have made life viable. The routine of my days was simple. At night I slept not at all. I would read until the dawn, then wake the entire family by putting on a record of the slow movement of Rachmaninov's Second Concerto.

My brothers would come down the stairs in varying states of grunting rage, wishing to hang Rachmaninov and flog me. I would sleep for about an hour then walk the hill-top paths for two hours, talking to myself, or the sheep, or composing in my mind the next chapter of my first novel. By the time I returned to the house the chapter was ready to be decanted on to paper as fast as my sixpenny fountain pen could travel.

The novel was not written in the customary vacuum. Victor Gollancz had advertised a competition for the best novel on unemployment. I felt that as far as this problem was concerned I was the national dipstick. Industrially the valley had the rattle in its throat and I was making some pretty good sounds myself. The book's title was *Sorrow For Thy Sons*, which, against the background of my general mood, was almost cheerful. It had a few good suicides, some inept sex and plenty of hunger.

Wynne typed it for me. He had bought a small typewriter and worked flat on his back in bed with the typewriter on his chest. This did not help the novel very much. Looking like a pair of hashish smugglers Wynne and I slipped the untidy package into the post office. The police, who were whipping up a small Red scare, put their ears to it for possible ticking.

Gollancz said he liked the fervour of the book, but its facts were so raw, its wrath so pitiless, its commercial prospects were nil unless he could issue a free pair of asbestos underdrawers to every reader. So he had to say no to publication. But he would like me to come and have a word with him in London about other possibilities. I took eleven shillings from my nearly exhausted private hoard and took a cheap day-return to London. I spent my last sixpence on cigarettes at Paddington and walked to Henrietta Street, a sad stroll even when life is chuckling. I got to the stairs, a gloomy flight if ever I saw one, that led to Gollancz's office. I lost resolution and fled back to Paddington and home.

That sort of antic has been a theme of my stay on this earth. I get close to an event, I hear it breathe, then, like any panto-mime sorcerer, I vanish. Much later Gollancz was to publish ten of my novels, but never once did I climb those stairs. In terms of self-exclusion my eyes have always beaten Dante's to the draw.

Most evenings of that post-Oxford year I spent in cinemas, which rounded out the note of alienation admirably. The valley teemed with cinemas, so there was always a new programme to check on. Even to someone like myself for whom the cinema was not an art but a way of darkness and insulation, the films struck one as patchy. The British cinema was providing an ample X-ray of the asinine clowns and immoralists who were leading us into the butcher's shop.

In the American films there were hints of validity. The Roosevelt influence had brought Hollywood as near to a gravelly truthfulness as it will ever come. The cinema seats were cheap; one could indulge oneself endlessly. Comfort came rarely. For twopence one sat on cement, for threepence on wood, for fourpence on plush. On the bitterest winter nights, in the least heated halls, one could always, with a little coaxing, get some careless smoker to set one alight.

Then the dark lotus year was ended. I found I had four shillings and sixpence left in the bank. I walked to the bank. I was more than ever impressed by the thickness of its doors and appalled at the prospect of entering into any transaction over those massive counters involving so absurdly small a sum. I turned away. The money is still there, probably puzzling some earnest accountant and keeping Britain steady with its tiny but loyal ring of confidence in the bankers.

I made my way to the bridge in the middle of the town. I leaned against the parapet. Its steel was no harder than my dilemma. I was penniless, unfitted for entry into any market and overdue at the grave. I had been sure that the final crushing of my nest-egg would coincide with the climax of my nervous exhaustion, the collapse of my will. I was in a mood to do something defiantly Roman, like throwing myself into the river. But that tactic at the time was being overworked and in personal conduct I always aimed at a bit of distinction. Besides, the river was running shallow and the valley was full of voters who recovered from their anguish as soon as they touched the waters and came walking out of the stream without impediment, and giving out false explanations of how they came to be dripping wet. The only other alternative was a walk to the North Pole. I had always been attracted by the idea of a gradual, lethal numbness and a long absence of daylight.

I was picking over these notions when my brother-in-law Charles, the doctor, pulled up alongside me. He had not seen me for a couple of years. I had had a ferocious wrangle with him on some point of social philosophy. He had become a brisk Malthusian in the course of his work among a fair number of dirt-spoiled and witless families. He had come to the valley from several years of medical work on ocean liners and in the American West. He had reacted badly to the strident untidiness of our gulch. His imagination seemed to inhabit a world of quick lice, dull eyes and slow tongues. When we tried to drag his attention to what we thought clear examples of intelligence and valour, flanked by plenty of soap, he told us to wipe our eyes and take another look. He had several hard notions for the pruning of humanity, and it was clear from his eyes as that evening ended that he had me singled out for a healing touch of the shears.

But there was no coldness in his thoughts that day on the bridge. He was shocked by the sight of me, the gauntness of my cheeks, the skeletal bareness of my frame, the general impression of a life perversely hastening into sunset. He had me lodged in hospital for three months, arranged for the surgical reduction of my thyroid and a modest extension of my life-span.

When I came back into the world the years of frenzy were finished. My jungle juices had been thinned out. The pressures that had driven my mind in and out of storm-clouds had been eased. I had been brought back to something like normal, and it was a peculiar feeling: utter sobriety after a long, cheap jag.

The next four years were spent in some of the most confusing bits of social work ever recorded. I volunteered for the Spanish war, but the local organisers made it plain that the presence of an enfeebled eccentric in a crusading brigade would do nothing but brace Franco. I lectured interminably to unemployed men in shacks they called Social Settlements, and I had to adjust my idiom and dialectical pace to the fact that the hall would empty as soon as it stopped raining.

I spent a few months in what I still regard as the most septically depressing place I shall ever know. It was a camp for the rehabilitation of the unemployed in the middle of what I imagined to be an area of reclaimed bogland in Staffordshire. The camp's real aim was to house German prisoners in the forthcoming war. I was one of the education officers. One of the items was the making of firm knots in rope, but this was dropped when it was found that the brighter pupils would go out and hang themselves as soon as they mastered a knot in which they had real confidence.

The place was visited twice or three times a week by the area administrator, an ex-machine-gun officer from the first world war. He was a man being driven mad by a waning sex-potency, a stout nymphomaniac for a wife, an unmoved bullet which had caused a cancerous degeneration of the jaw-bone, and a terrifying hatred of the job he was doing and the men who were its raw material. He would watch them shuffling about the compound in their nailed boots and lead-heavy corduroy trousers. They had been unemployed for periods of no less than five years, and their physical condition was deplorable. At the sight of them the area administrator would whine, 'Not worth the powder to blow them to hell with.'

One afternoon he kept repeating this until I had to tell him, in a quiet but clear voice, not to be such a bloody fool. I was afraid his rage might have deafened him, that he had not heard. He had. He sacked me on the spot. If ever a temperament contrived the iron bars of a wretched fate it was that man's. As I moved for the last time through the avenue of fir-trees that led from the camp to the station, I knew what it would probably feel like to emerge from black waters in a crippled submarine.

From that winter of the heart I was moved to a part of Derbyshire where the collective intelligence was kept on so short a leash it almost silenced me for good. From there I went to the Manchester area, notably Rochdale. The wartime black-out had started. Rochdale square was a maze of spiked railings standing about six inches from the ground, an aid to darkness if ever there was one. I spent most of my night hours tripping over these things and being hoisted up by policemen. This happened so often the police decided before I left that at last they had found a really fundamental social worker.

Thinking to fire-proof myself against the furnaces to come, I volunteered for the Field Security Corps, a rudimentary spying outfit. I was interviewed by an officer whose French was worse than mine; he had been practising his errors longer. He asked me what, in the likely event of my failing to enter the Field Security, I might fancy as an alternative in a military way. I said, 'Tanks.' He asked me why. I told him that in an overplanned age a tank might give one a choice of direction. He said something in French about cowardice being the mother and mistress of all corruptions. I agreed.

I was examined by doctors. They decided that my buckled nerves and wretched reflexes put me beyond the range of gunfire unless the Government, for reasons of their own, decided to shoot me anyway.

The war grew noisier. When I heard my first air-raid warning, despite all the efforts of my wife to calm me, I rushed on to the landing and went down the stairs with both my legs in one leg of my trousers. I hurt my skull and gashed my hand against the front door. The following night I saw the whole of Piccadilly, a square in central Manchester, ablaze with incendiary bombs. There must have been thirty to forty buildings going up in flames. A fire-tender from a nearby town called Middleton careered into the square. A fireman jumped off, keyed up to somewhere beyond concert pitch and asked me, 'Where's t' fire?' For the millionth time in my life I could not think of a full answer.

I wanted a cloister, a school, something quiet and timeless, something antithetical to the world's statesmen and sergeants. I found it. A Grammar School in Cardigan, West Wales, where I was to teach French and Spanish to University level for a wage that has already passed into a social footnote: four pounds a week.

I spent my first night in Cardigan in a most genial pub, talking loosely about the war and finishing the evening being warned

by a special policeman to stop spreading alarm and despon-
dency. Then he winked and brought me a beer. An ambiguous
place altogether.

The next morning I walked up the main street of the town to
begin a couple of decades of teaching grammar.

3
It might have been the resonance. It could have been the wine

Mr Walford is a man caught in my thoughts. Especially so when I read journals of education or listen to Speech Days, in which one hears a full subfusc flood of stuff about the love and dedication that a teacher gives his charges. Neanderthal man would have given about as much dedication and love to his task as Mr Walford.

He had come from some small village in the valley of the Cothi in Carmarthen, West Wales. In spirit he never left there. Fishing, bee-keeping, woodcraft were the things that filled his brain. The school and the industrial area in which it was located he viewed as a squalid impertinence. He regarded rate-subsidised education as a passing fad from which he derived a salary he privately considered to be absurdly high. He continued to serve as a teacher and to draw his pay because he had, by some curious chance, been educated to graduation standard, and he was too devotedly mean to quit before his full pension rate had matured.

H

His father had been a rural craftsman, a great maker of coracles. Most of Mr Walford's thinking was pitched on a nostalgia for what the coracle represented: a clean quiet stream, a craft for which no great expense or inhuman power was required, an approach to salmon so guileful and gentle that it made their death nice and acceptable.

He was the most obdurate exile I have ever known. His impatience with the subjects and boys he taught was total. His beat was general science and he must have found the stink and artifices of the laboratories abhorrent. He might have had a slight and casual contact with one of the Welsh chapels in the town but even that perished abruptly. When they stepped up the collections to meet the needs of an insatiable fabric fund he lapsed into some kind of agnostic impassivity. Apart from a vague pantheism and a consuming belief in manual work and thrift, I do not think he had a formal philosophy. Of orthodox Christian doctrine he would have had about as much as Magwa the Mohican.

He regarded me as something of a freak. He had an idea that I had had something to do with the sulphurous stirrings of the thirties, and, in one of his odd, avuncular moments, he told me not to be such a fool. Leave governments alone, he said. Don't protest. Stay quiet and they'd pass you by. Get rid of one lot and another pack of clowns and rodneys would take their place. If they came near with a demand or a request, just hide.

It was exactly as if his whole being were encompassed in a dark forest and through the forest were coming an evil, rather foolish, predatory beast. Don't fight it, don't try to deceive it or cajole. Stay still, hidden, and it will forget about you and go. He kept reminding me of the legend of the '*pobl bach ddu*', the squat, small aboriginal people who took to the hill-tops and caves in order to get away from the invading Celts.

When he heard that I had been one of the field-workers on those researches into social gloom on which the Beveridge blueprint of the social welfare state was based, his limbs moved as if he had been shot. From then on he regarded me as responsible

for most of the waste he saw around him. The average pupil in
the school he saw as a creature whose mental faculties and gifts
our sort of training would surely destroy.

'Thomas,' he would say, 'you shouldn't have helped that
Beveridge. All help corrupts swiftly. State help corrupts fastest
of all.'

There were times when his disgust with the town and school
overwhelmed him. The first symptoms would be a tendency to
leave the laboratory in which he was teaching, whatever the rac-
ket being made by the young scientists, and to stare at a meadow
which led up to the hills that backed the school to the north.
During his free periods he would have to relax completely to
keep his malaise below the point at which he would have to
pull up stakes and make tracks for the west. He would take two
chairs in the staff-room and lie immobile on them, a fair por-
tion of his long body quite unsupported except by some bit of
Carmarthen or Yogi guile. He could give you a fright if you
blundered into the room expecting nothing more abnormal than
the sight of a colleague turning his back on his marking and
having a quiet smoke up the chimney.

I do not recall seeing Mr Walford read a book. His notes, if
ever he used such, belonged to his student period and were con-
sidered to have stopped short at Humphry Davy, a sample of
whose safety lamp he had in his cupboard, and which he some-
times showed to the boys in the aftermath of a visit by inspectors
who wanted the whole caper of teaching to be dramatic and
vivid. He could also talk with relish about certain industrial
diseases whose origins had some clinical interest. Blindness
caused by ammonia in those whose work had to do with cess-
pits; fosse-jaw, milkman's limp and tinker's toe.

He had made little effort to check on the new wisdoms that
had spurted out of the great savageries of our time. Rutherford
he had heard of but did not believe. Einstein he wrote off as a
mischief-maker. In any case he drew back from any name that
was not manifestly British. His interest in general ideas was not
more kindly. Once, when excited by a double helping of prunes
in the school dining hall, I tried to explain to him how certain

contemporary novelists in a practical and admirable way had tried to illumine and then to shift some morbid stoppages in the veins of our social anatomy. Every mishap in human relationship, I said, from war down to a gruff, parental clip on the ear was really a thrombotic breakdown of sympathetic perception.

He looked at me as if he would have liked to have me at the business end of a coracle paddle.

'You get all that stuff from that Beveridge,' he said. 'Forget it. Most men are nuisances. If they come towards you, hide. An otter I'd like to have been. They're fast and fit and don't need a licence to fish. Plop they go and just try to find them. Try explaining to otters about that Beveridge.'

He reached a top note on this theme whenever it was his turn to supervise dinner duty. He never said a grace, for he saw nothing that God or man needed to be proud of in the sight of five hundred boys crowded around a state-provided trough, when they could just as well have been taking their fill from hand-picked herbs on the hill behind the school.

One morning I went into the staff-room and found Mr Walford busy. He had a fairly long staff of wood and on to this he was attaching a massive skirt of stiff twigs by means of a tin hoop. At first I thought he was fashioning some rough instrument, a variant of the birch, with which he intended to play hell with the more loutish of his fifth form, a coarse, violent lot, the first ruddy fruit of the black-out. Then I saw that it resembled a brush and I thought that Mr Walford meant to clean the chimney. We had in that room the most blockable set of flues in the school, but then I remembered that Mr Walford had no objection to smoke-filled rooms, had indeed been suspected of ramming rags up the chimney and crippling the cowl to bring the smoking to full volume, and encouraged some of his colleagues to use the other staff-rooms.

'What's this, Thomas?' he said, holding up the bit of handicraft.

'It looks like a brush.'

'That's it. It's a broom, a rustic broom. Do you know there are people who buy brushes from shops?'

I had bought a brush the day before, but I was not going to commit myself in front of Mr Walford.

'They buy them. And all they need is a bit of stick, a few twigs and they've got a perfect broom. Look how it works.'

He worked the broom up and down the fairly dusty floor and seemed to leave the dust unharmed. 'My wife would never dream of using anything but these. You can only ensure full cleanliness with a natural type of bristle.'

I knew from my wife that Mrs Walford, a woman full of what the Spaniards would call a fine and genial irony, made a great play of using the broom in front of Mr Walford but as soon as his back was turned made instant use of a great battery of commercially produced brushes which she kept in a locked closet.

He gave me the besom to study. He could see from my face that even if I admired the deftness of its making it was not going to make me give up reading. He looked worried.

'Could you make one of those things, Thomas?'

'No. I'm poor with twigs.'

'Well, you'd better learn.' He waved his arm to take in the whole school. 'These places aren't going to last for ever, you know. This is just a passing foolery, going to colleges and saying things you don't want to say in classrooms that I never wanted built to boys who don't want to hear. A passing foolery. But dirt will be with us to the end and where there's dirt someone will want to brush it.'

He motioned me to sit down and got me a new pole and a handful of twigs. Then, instructed by him, I started to make the only brush on earth that had bristles all the way to the top of the handle. He did not want to discourage me.

'Just the job if you're lying flat on the floor,' he said.

*

In his youth Mr Walford had been a notable athlete. He was a hurdler and he put his phenomenal ability as a runner and a jumper down to nights of evasive action down west in flight from gamekeepers and landlords. He had been one of the British Olympic team that went to Athens in the early years of the century. That had been his only trip abroad. It had left no light or joy in his mind.

One morning, our classics man, Mr Selley, who had been to Greece the summer before on a fruit-carrying freighter, held himself spellbound describing aloud, through a whole free period, the dark blue loveliness of the Aegean, the petrified world-mind of the Parthenon, the dusty pathos of eroded hills and frustrated heroes, who lived in poverty and desolation far below the last gleam of the Homeric sun.

In the staff-room with Mr Selley were Mr Walford and myself. Mr Walford, who felt himself betrayed if he were not doing something with his hands, was trying to repair a chair from which a leg had broken loose. He seemed not to be heeding Mr Selley's message.

I, eager to be well in with both sides, was nodding hard at Mr Selley and also assuring Mr Walford that the chair was going to be better than ever. Mr Walford was pleased with the interest I was taking and invited me to take two experimental whacks at the chair with the cricket bat he was using as a hammer. In five seconds I had brought the chair back to its original base of ruin.

Mr Selley was not pleased with what was happening to his audience. He had always been convinced that in our company the Greeks were speaking to a poor ear. The only Greeks we knew in our town were ship-chandlers and they seemed to be doing all right and did not seem to give the sliver of a commercial damn whether Homer or the sun gleamed or not.

'But then,' said Mr Selley, 'you people wouldn't understand. If you've not been to Greece, if you've not seen the Acropolis, Mount Athos where the monks are, if you've not heard the language of Pericles spoken by living lips, you'd have no idea, you'd always prefer some witless bit of carpentry to a genuine glimpse of the glory that was Greece.'

'Mr Walford has been there,' I said. 'He was there, in Athens. He was a hurdler.'

Mr Selley looked startled, as if he imagined that Mr Walford had started hurdling in a general way from West Wales, had got as far as Athens, seen his mistake and hurdled back again.

'He was an Olympic athlete,' I said. 'He was in Athens.'

Mr Selley put his hand on the shoulder of Mr Walford, who was trying to ram the chair leg into a hole that seemed to have become twice the size as the result of my hammering.

'Then, Mr Walford, you've had the most golden privilege that can befall a man,' said Mr Selley.

'What did you think of the Greeks, Mr Walford?' I asked.

'Not much,' he said, and he raised the chair leg aloft as if he thought it would be easier if he now tried to fit the thing into me. 'Not much. I didn't look very closely. I wasn't there long. I was glad to come away. Dirty, I thought. They'd got the wrong sort of deacons, I think.'

But Mr Walford kept up his interest in athletics. He was the supreme official at the annual sports. For a week before the event he would have platoons of boys rolling out the chains that marked the official distances. It was traditional that these boys should be the most torpid reckoners in school, and given this chance to see mathematics in living action.

The lesson never came off. Within half an hour Mr Walford would be like a callow Egyptian overseer in thrall to a band of malicious Israelites. Any chain that Mr Walford would order to be stiffened became instantly serpentine, and the measuring session would end with Mr Walford and his helpers as helplessly corralled as sheep in the middle of the field.

Mr Walford would curse quietly in Welsh, uncoil himself, and order the starting and finishing points for the various events to be marked wherever the whitewash chanced to fall. This made some records easier to break; others more difficult. All in all we broke even.

On sports day Mr Walford was the official starter. For this he had one of the longest and most erratic guns ever used for a peacetime purpose. It had the heavy, ugly look of an eighteenth-century flintlock, and Mr Walford seemed to have as much control over it as he had over the weather. As often as not when

starting a race he would hold the gun in the air and keep work-
ing away at the trigger without producing a sound, while the
crouched runners either went into a long-distance cramp or
crept out of the race. But between races the gun seemed to be
going off constantly. Mr Walford would stop to explain to
somebody why the gun had failed to go off and every time he
lifted the gun to explain why there would be an explosion.

My own part in these sports meetings was minimal. My habit
of lapsing into an uncritical boredom at the sight of any sport-
ing activity made me useless as a judge of events in which
people tended to move swiftly from one point to another. There
was one sports day on which I was to serve as one of the judges
of the junior and senior walking races. For this the judges
needed neither great acuity nor theoretical background. Just
spot any boy who was overtly running and pull him out.

Mr Walford had been a race walker until well into middle
age, and he knew the rules for this event very well. When he
had the time he would stand by me and point out the boys who
were breaking the heel-and-toe rule, and I would frown at these
boys and call them off the track.

The junior race began. In the judges' box next to mine there
was a fussy and expert official wearing a red blazer with a badge
the size and colour of an average Nantgarw plate, the emblem
of a noted harriers' team of long ago. When judging the human
dilemma, the place that most people would ascribe to the class
system, racial spite and original sin, this man awarded to slack-
ness among judges at athletic meetings. At previous sports he
had reported me to Mr Walford for apparent somnambulism.
He was not a staff-member. He was invited as an authority and
there was not much one could do about him.

The junior walkers entered on the second of their three laps.
Between my interest in Mr Walford's gun and my absorption
in one of the young walkers who, between loose elastic in his
knicks and a naturally poor stance, was walking in all respects
like a duck, I did not have much of an eye for transgressors.

But the judge in the next box, the expert, was on top form,
and he was weeding out three or four competitors every time

the field passed him. He shouted over to me that at any time I cared to pay some attention to the event I would see boys sprinting past me, and that the only boys really walking were boys worn out by running.

I made a vow to be more alert for the senior event. For a minute I gave a monkish concentration to the styles of these older competitors. The leading boy at the end of the first lap was moving so fast I decided he could not possibly be walking, so I pulled him out. The boy turned out to be the son of the man in the red blazer and a perfect specimen of race walker. Had it been dark I am sure the man in the red blazer would have left me for the vultures. As it was he just came up to me and said to me, in a voice that came right up from the bottom of his badge, that he was preparing a lampoon about me for the journal of the Athletic Association.

This upset me, for one does not like to be made to look a fool or a dunce before schoolboys. The man in the red blazer had made his judgment of me as private as that horn which ushers in the druids at the eisteddfod. And the incident of my pulling out the only competitor of the afternoon who was working strictly within the rules had spread around the field.

I went over to Mr Walford, who stood in the middle of the field fondling his silent gun. He was wearing an ancient hat of Mexican breadth. It and the gun gave him the look of a very conservative sheriff.

My first impulse was to demand that he debar or defrock the man in the red blazer and make a move to eliminate walking races from the curriculum. But I could see that he was in no mood to be bothered by any subordinate topics. With my luck that day, the man in the red blazer would probably turn out to be his brother.

'How is it going?' I asked.

'Everything is going except the gun,' he said. 'But never mind. It was tending to shake my teeth whenever it made any sort of an explosion at all, and I don't want to squander money on a more secure set before I die. I have a wooden contrivance in school that will do the job as well as this weapon. A sort of

clapper. Makes a loud, dry noise. Tends to scare the lights out
of those runners who are crouched in the tighter type of pos-
ture, but it'll do.'

He came as near as he ever would to laughing, and in a sur-
prising fit of friendliness threw around my shoulder the arm
that held the gun. As soon as the gun touched my back the
mechanism sprang to life, and I had a powder stain from the
small of my back down to my shoes. From that day on I have
never crossed over the rope that divides the public from judges
and athletes.

*

Most of us will go to our end with a fur of mysteries upon
us. The thickest and most maddening of those mysteries will be
the urge of some people to censor, diminish or destroy the de-
lights of other people.

In this field no impulse works with more success and mis-
chief than that of written propaganda in favour of sensual
frankness and enthusiasm.

I am happy to say that my own experience in this matter is
slight. Whenever my curiosity about some especially salacious
work has been aroused by the publicity of a lawsuit and I make
my way to a bookshop, a posse of policemen, toting away a few
crates of the condemned works for burning, meets me at the
door.

Now and then I have been impressed by the profits made by
the near pornography that thrives in the Private Eye and Secret
Agent belts. But I am stuck in a groove of social earnestness and
in my fiction there will be little scope for the swaggering male
predator and the ardent concubine. A mild kiss against the
warmest wall of the local bakehouse, perhaps, but even that will
be followed by a chastening round of debate in one of the ante-
rooms of the local Welfare Hall on some such subject as 'That
we regard Bulldog Drummond as a corrupt and disastrous
loon'.

Only once did I come anywhere near inclusion in the magic

circle of writers whose names are mentioned with a wink and an excited nod. It was when my ancient colleague, Mr Walford, discovered years late that I had become a novelist. Mr Walford had, in his life, read little fiction. As a young scientist in the nineties he had broken his teeth on the slower type of text, usually second-hand and torn into a vexing distortion.

As a young Christian he had had his mind chafed by volumes of interminable memoirs by the distinguished pastors of our land who had plenty of time and things to remember. His father had been a compulsive buyer of these tomes, and when he got home after a jag in the local bookstall he was so crazy with regret at having spent so much he would make Mr Walford read them as well.

Mr Walford's mind hung on to the details of these books of reminiscence with the tenacity of the Pinkertons, and he could bore the ears off you with conversations culled from a thousand droning manses. There was, most of us agreed, an element of sadism in this, for no one, not even Mr Walford, could have communicated so much tedium through any kind of interest in what was being communicated.

In his later years his main reading was an Agricultural Gazette, from which he would occasionally read some opaque message about the operation of the Seeds Act of 1919 or the vagaries of milk profits around Llandeilo. He also received free copies of the local paper, published in the township of his birth, which always contained in any given week so many incidents of sexual daring in places like cow-byres, we often asked whether this platoon of immoralists did not constitute a knock to the dairy trade in his natal zone.

'No,' he said. 'They strike a kind of balance. They live close to nature there. Not like you lot here.'

Of fiction Mr Walford read hardly anything at all. He claimed that life as lived socially was about eighty per cent falsehood, and he did not see the point of having paid story-tellers adding to the pyramid of delusion. He would sometimes say that he had a small library in his home. He had asked someone to take it away but that had been fifteen years ago, and he assumed that the man had either forgotten or opted for illiteracy.

For novelists Mr Walford had no time. He had never met one and would never do anything to favour their existence. He had read a few bits of widescreen piety like *Uncle Tom, Ben Hur* and *The Robe*, but he did not associate these with any act of individual authorship. He saw them as the fruits of some collective goodness, and he thanked the memory of his mother for having been put in touch with them.

He saw the army of novel-writers in general as a malignant crew, freed by the very oddity of their calling into the paths of indecency.

'As a countryman,' he would say, 'I favour short, simple, cheap kinds of communication. Those novelists, all that writing. . . . No wonder their minds get bent. No wonder their dreams are in and out of bedrooms, and so on. Of course, I don't read such books. My own library is modest but each volume has to pass a high laundry test. All my books are clean as mountain springs, fresh as morning mint. *Treasure Island, The Road Mender, Cloister on the Hearth* and two of my childhood favourites, *Jim Blackwood, Jockey* and *Scenes from the Life of an Old Armchair*, both strong and telling statements against drink.'

In the matter of pornography Mr Walford was vigorously partisan. He had only the vaguest idea of what constituted pornography, but he had given a fair sector of his mind to it and he was against it, root and crop. Whenever he read a newspaper item describing the seizure and burning of a banned book, he drank an extra cup of tea during the morning break and puzzled people by shaking hands with them to celebrate another victory for the laved morality of his natal kitchen.

It was five years after the appearance of my first novel that Mr Walford learned that I had any connection with this craft. The discovery was one of several shocks that had hit Mr Walford almost simultaneously.

He had found that one staff-member played cards at home for money; another kept a sufficient number of wine bottles to qualify as a cellar and to mark him as a sot. A third colleague was contemplating divorce. Each of these revelations had snatched some garment of assurance from Mr Walford and hurt his flesh.

One morning he came up to me. His face was ravaged with concern.

'You write books then,' he said, and he made it sound as if I had been selling orphans on the open market.

I nodded.

'Grammar books?' he asked hopefully.

'No, novels.'

He limped off to sprinkle boracic on this fresh burn. The following day he took up the topic again.

'About those books. Is there anything immoral in them?'

'Oh no. Just about as sexless as can be. Maybe not as wholesome as *Jim Blackwood, Jockey*, but my characters just talk until they have purged themselves of everything but a mental unease about being together on the same earth in the same plot.'

Mr Walford went away to work that out. He came back five minutes later and I could see that he had failed to find the key to my sentence.

'But why novels?' he asked, and he sounded so chafed and petulant I gathered he would have been less put out if I had joined the other delinquent colleagues on the cards, wine and carnality front.

'Well,' I said, 'a novel is as good a basket as any for dumping the litter of a lifetime.'

He walked warily around that trope. It was clear that he was looking hard at his lifetime and finding no trace of litter. Then he smiled as broadly as if he were about to give me his heart and the deeds of his house.

'I'll read one of your novels,' he said. 'Don't think I've got a closed mind. It's not gaping but it's not closed. I'm just worried in case you've written something you'd be ashamed to read aloud in front of your mother.'

For several weeks he tried to borrow a copy of one of my books. Then he made his big decision.

'I'm going to buy a copy,' he said. 'Just to prove that I'm

ready to be foolhardy in the cause of tolerance.'

Two days later he came up to me during the tea-break and whispered in my ear, 'I've come to the bit about the white raincoat.' He blinked and walked swiftly away.

For a few moments I was foxed. I had to go back to the book to be reminded of the incident that had made Mr Walford take to whispering. It was innocent enough. Being a man with a long-term dread of rheumatism, when I had two of my characters together on a mountain-top during a rainy spell I wanted to put in a cautious word against the folly of sitting or lying on naked grass. I had arranged a white raincoat between the humans and the possibility of pneumonia.

The next day Mr Walford was at my ear again. 'I've finished that bit about the mountain-top and the mac. And I've got to tell you. Your book is definitely going behind my other books to join *The Blue Lagoon*.'

'But I didn't think you had any literature of that kind.'

When he replied his voice was shaking with protest. 'If it wasn't for you and your old white mac and black imagination you'd never have known, would you?'

And off he went, less sure of his direction than he had been for thirty years.

*

'An athlete's end can be a slow and sad affair,' said Mr Walford.

I agreed with him. His own achievements on the track as a runner and walker had been redoubtable. He had taken up race-walking to taper off from running when he had been told of the dangers of fatty heart, and so on, that threaten athletes when they give up violent action too abruptly. He could not think of anything to taper off on from walking, so he kept at it and by the time he was fifty he was the oldest and thinnest race walker in the region.

He adhered to a stern code of training. He told me that if ever, in sleep, he found his mind headed for any type of voluptuous fancy that might waste his energy or mar his dedication he would spring from bed, put his brow against the cold glass of the window and sing all the verses of Cardinal Newman's 'Lead Kindly Light', a cooling and cautionary item.

At week-ends he would walk, at top speed, fifteen miles on Saturday and twenty on Sunday, when he really had the feel of the road beneath his feet. For these outings he wore only a mustard-coloured pair of tight knicks. I believe he wore no vest because he considered the enormous, painful convulsions of his chest had a good chastening effect on the public. I don't know about the public. They chastened me.

He used the main roads and it was easily within his power to shoot past the slower buses. It was always interesting to watch the faces of the passengers on these buses when they got their first full view of Mr Walford in this rig, panting and looking quite crazed as he drove his almost nothing of a body on to higher levels of endurance. I heard more than one person ask how and when fakirs and dervishes had been admitted into the fold of Welsh nonconformity. And the phrase 'Good God, Gandhi!' uttered when Mr Walford began streaking away into the distance, could always count on an easy laugh.

When Mr Walford's mother was ill in an infirmary at Cardiff it was said that he combined training and family piety. His wife would go into Cardiff on the bus, with Mr Walford's suit, shirt, shoes and hat in a case. She would stand at the top of that underground toilet near the castle. Mr Walford, in just his knicks, would follow, no more than a few yards behind the bus and becoming annoyed every time the driver halted to take him on.

Mr Walford would snatch the case from his wife's hand and, without a pause for any acknowledgment, would go like a flash down the steps of the convenience, a penny in his hand. He would let himself into one of the closets and come out in one or two minutes, fully dressed.

The first few times he did this, the curator of the convenience, who saw only parts of this whole manœuvre, was convinced that the gloomy, enclosed nature of his trade now had him seeing a naked man who dropped in at the speed of light and then vanished into thin air. The curator, a conscientious man, thought that in the context this set an unwholesome precedent. When he got at the truth, the curator spoke severely to Mr Walford and he was obliged in future to greet the curator with a warning shout from the top of the steps, and walk slowly down, smiling, before entering the closet. This made the whole thing seem less fey.

Another thing that struck the eye of Mr Walford in his training sessions was the number of times he seemed to surprise lovers in the full shout of passion. Since he trained in rubber shoes and put such little pressure on them he gave no warning of his coming, and he stumbled over so many wooers who were given no chance to sit up and get straight, he began to see the world as one immense sexual circus. This strengthened the fierce Calvinism of his early days.

'If rain has a source,' he would tell me, 'then it ought to be found. And when found, into it should be poured a bulky load of bromide. The mortal heat that will give mankind its ultimate scorch has nothing to do with super-bombs. What fluorine in tap-water has done for teeth, bromide in the rain-water could do for morals. My mind is a moving picture of this age's turpitude. I'm like the eye of a first-class conscience. I move too fast for anything to be concealed. There are couples about here who've seen me leap over them so often they must think I come as part of a package deal with the whole business of affection.'

In his middle fifties the wind of physical ambition in Mr Walford died down. He took to walking slowly about the school, as if he were moving along the crumbling edge of a cliff. And indeed much of life had come to appear unsafe and unlikable to him. It would seem that his spirit had been kept spinning and bright by the super-normal speeds at which he had once run and walked. Now his most settled source of content was to walk up and down the empty corridors, coming out with recessive and dispiriting sentences like the one about an athlete's end being a sad and slow affair.

His most frequent companion on these ambles was myself,

for I was about the only person who looked upon him as a serious and admirable bit of human experience. He rarely used the staff-rooms now, for he found in the talk of the new recruits overtones of slick banter that put him off his mental stroke.

In the last four or five years before his retirement Mr Walford became a fanatical bee-keeper. He often told me that he hoped one day to bring his technique to such a point of smoothness he would be able to direct a whole swarm of hostile bees at any class in school that got on his nerves, and that, by the end, covered the whole age-range.

I often met him in the countryside around the town wearing a long brown coat which he kept for his traffic with bees, and a kind of large helmet of fine wire mesh. He fancied himself in this article and when his naturally hard, high voice came filtering through it, it had an unsettling effect on people that pleased him.

Once, on a bus taking us home, he kept the helmet on, saying that it gave him a nice sense of remoteness and struck a note of repulsion which would curb the noisy blitheness of the other passengers. He created a certain panic when someone suggested that Mr Walford was dressed like this because he knew there was a swarm waiting to board the bus two stops on. He lifted his helmet and denied this in a voice that had to be believed.

Once, when he was brooding about the honey of which he had a surplus, I gave him a book that dealt with the ancient mead, its making and use. He set up some kind of primitive still and he told me the stuff was flowing at a fairly brisk rate, but he did not invite anyone to share a sip of it with him.

'Of course,' he said, 'I'm not less against the drink now than I was when I was a boy. Twice, before the age of sixteen, I strained my voice shouting abuse at arrant drunkards and singing bits of dry propaganda through the letter boxes of citizens active in the licensed trade. But I can't connect any product of bees with sin and that's that. I think there's some kind of rebirth in this mead. I've read too many accounts of Celtic and Viking warriors still swinging their axes and desires about at

I

the age of ninety and more, all on account of being waist deep in mead most of their lives. I fancy a bit of rebirth. You can't imagine an athlete like me slipping willingly down a paralysed declension to death. One of these days I'll drink the vital cup of mead that'll bring the sun up brilliantly once again over my darkened blood.'

But I saw no sign of renascence. If anything he walked a little more slowly, his eyes down, as if there was a point just in front of him which he did not want to see or recognise.

Mr Walford's departure from the school and town was firmly consistent. A heart seizure, brought on by all that walking, had made him even more angular and fractious, even more manic about having betrayed himself when he moved in early man-hood from the west and the riverside farm where he had been born.

The school wanted to make a collection and some sort of presentation to him. He said no. He had never, he said, done anything to merit a collection of money among boys. There was no point in their trying to move him to a mood of affection he had never naturally felt. It was suggested that he make a fare-well speech in the main hall. He said no. His level, oratorically, was that of the bees on which he had doted. A short, unfriendly buzz and that would be that. No speech. What about a modest valedictory tea in the school canteen? He had never, he said, agreed with the school canteen. So that was out. He was quite withdrawn now. He had even given his bees away months be-fore. He spoke no more of mead, of a new sunrise in the veins, of warriors undimmed by a century of life.

For the whole of the last week of his last term he was absent from school. He made it known he did not want to be visited. On the Thursday he sent me a note, asking me to pick up the few books on his shelf in the staff-room and to bring them to him on the Friday evening. 'And don't wait for the door to open. Come in. I'll be upstairs.'

I went along. I pushed the front door open. The occasion had a flavour. No other member of the staff had been inside Mr Walford's house before. The place was musty and in militant

disarray. Mr Walford had lived alone for years. It was as if he
had been trying to make the face of his loneliness as ugly and
contemptible as he could, to avenge himself on some tyranny
of tidiness that had made him ache in the days when his family
had been about him.

I stood on the landing. I called out. There was no answer. I
tried two doors. The rooms were bare. I thought at first that
Mr Walford might have fled and bequeathed me this experience
of being quite alone in a ruin as a bonus. The third room I tried
was furnished, but with no sign of Mr Walford. The paper of
one whole wall had fallen away and covered the bed like a
canopy. I lifted the paper, as tense as Schliemann in Crete break-
ing through to those regal death-masks. Mr Walford lay there,
still as a mummy. He moved his lips faintly, in welcome, as
unperturbed as if, all his life, he had been used to seeing his
visitors appear beneath a pall of wallpaper. He pointed to a
corner cupboard.

'There's one last bottle of mead in there,' he said. 'Fetch it.'

I fetched it. He allowed himself a short toast before he drank
his first glass.

'To all the things that went away and had the sense never to
return.'

We drank the rest of the bottle in complete silence. He raised
a finger in grave dismissal.

'I'll fix that paper back for you,' I said. 'Looks sinister, in-
decent.'

'No, that's all right. Quite cosy. Good view.'

I found a hammer and nails. The mead had spoiled my aim
and if Mr Walford hadn't asked me, for pity's sake, to go and
leave him to recuperate for tomorrow's journey I would have
been through the bedroom wall. As I left the room I heard a
rustle and Mr Walford vanished again beneath his arc of paper.

The next morning he boarded, as a passenger, the rough-
riding lorry that was taking the last of his furniture back to his
natal cottage. I was the only one there to say goodbye to him as
the ancient engine started up. I believe I heard him say that he
would be glad to see me any time I came west. But the engine

was shaking him like a major pulley and it might have been something quite different that he said. There was something in his eyes that said he considered me a last link and that he was, without a shadow of regret, breaking it.

Anyway, I never went and he never came back.

Within ten days of Mr Walford's departure, I left teaching myself. It was a sudden decision. I was still twenty years away from any kind of pension and, the way I felt, about twenty hours away from lunacy.

On my last day at the school I lost my temper utterly with a group of refractory lads to whom I was teaching elementary French. Culturally they were pulling out of continental Europe, a kind of sullen academic Dunkirk, and I was in no mood to wave them back. I did a kind of demented dance before them. At the lesson's end I repented every moment of bawling impatience I had ever been guilty of. The next class was to be my very last. I sat down in front of them and said not a word. I looked at them with sincere, radiant affection. Then I walked out of their lives, leaving them more confused than they had ever been before.

4
Move up. It's the albatross again

Early in the 1960s George Devine, Director of the Royal Court Theatre, wrote to me suggesting that I should write a play. George, now tragically dead, was one of the brightest spirits ever to walk through Britain's world of theatre. And he had had a very bright idea. It was to stop relying on the group of known playwrights, to break away from the stage on which butlers and romantic contrivance and coincidence out-creaked each other, and drag in writers from an ampler, less crafty medium. So, fetch in the novelists; yank them off their sly or pampered backsides and set them communicating directly with a live audience.

The idea, of course, was doomed to fail on a magnificent scale. Novelists are solitary, rambling, untidy animals, rarely capable of devising any brief and pointed entertainment. But at that moment the idea sounded good and it seemed for a moment to work. Quite a number of audiences were found for novelists persuaded by the English Stage Company to assist in the renaissance of the spoken word, animating and making co-

gent characters normally dumb and detached. The sharp but
kindly frenzies of Sloane Square were going to chip away the
rust from men too long isolated and spoiled by the trick of pri-
vate gibbering, and reveal them to the world as a bunch of
shining prophets, a breed much needed in post-war Britain, and
we could have done with a modest dose of them in pre-war
Britain. If a genuinely shining prophet were to emerge in
Britain, before or after any war, I wonder under what regula-
tion they'd book him, for shining or prophesying. And they'd
probably be right to do so. Conscious utterance, in social
evolution, has never mattered the peeling of a damn. The rocks
did not harden on instruction, nor by that method will societies
improve. Errors rub together in the dark and any odd bit of
rightness that emerges does so by virtue of some sly bit of
partheno-genesis. In a community that makes such heavy ritual
of sanctifying morons anyone with an authentic gift for social
divination could not open his mouth without a paralysing sense
of farce.

I wrote my play without any great zeal. I was in no mood
for proffering messages to a visible public. My early delight in
belting away from a stage as alto or Christian polemicist had
worn thin. My nerve-ends were in ashes and my first philosophy
that had once chirped hope from every branch of its experience
had shed its leaves and evicted its singing guest. A few mut-
tered phrases in the porch, a garnering of the more livid items
of gossip in the pub, a few disgruntled remarks about the al-
most tangible silence that had formed around my novels, this
was about as far as I wished to go in public communication.

But in lurches I got the play written. I went easy on ideas,
having few around at the time. I played the field for a few gentle
laughs and could not, in anticipation, hear them coming. The
plot was a kind of extension of autobiography. It was an attempt
to imagine what my family life would have been if my brothers
and I had not been dispersed from our kitchen by the squalid
autumn of the thirties. The play shows a group of brothers, pro-
fessionally established in their town at fairly low levels, taking
their nicotine like captive mice and becoming even more

neurotic. The wallpaper patterns are uniformly of withered dreams. They are looked after by a gifted and compassionate sister who tries to assuage their futilities and galvanise their hearts. She gets nowhere. People of this sort make a loving collection of their own wounds. Keep them under glass, touch them in long sessions of self-amazement. Show them off and wonder when the Arts Council would give Masoch and Wales a break and make them a grant.

I had almost thrown the play to one side halfway through the last act. There was too much smell of the musty past about and even a man as hooked as I on obliquity felt I was not saying enough. I showed it to a friend. He read it caustically and with a frown that came south at a frightening pace. 'Sentimental,' he said. 'Basically simple-witted. Anybody preoccupied with the thought of laughter is bound to end up as a corrupt sort of bastard. That's you. Corrupt bastard.'

The way he said it, I believed it. I listened to my friend with less than my usual care.

'On this showing you are no more than two small cart-loads of bland bull away from the House of Lords. And you were the glib sod who was going to tell Maxim Gorki and Mayakovsky to move up. You, boy, are the graveyard of honest commitment in these disturbed times. But I'll say this. With this piece limping just behind Dickens' *Christmas Carol* and shaking crutches with Tiny Tim, you might make a bit of money out of it.'

This encouragement took me to the end of the play. I finished it and sent it off. It was the mention of money that got my will poised for action. I wanted to get out of teaching. I had grown so weak I had boys to help me carry the chalk along the longer corridors. My tongue dropped dead at the touch of a grammatical rule. The school itself seemed suddenly to have filled with boys wearing leather aprons of incredible size, and clearly bent on stressing the technical side and transforming the material world, and hoist mankind from the realm of necessity. If leather aprons and dedicated looks could do it, these were the boys.

When I slid the manuscript over the post-office counter, I did

it with so little ambition or hope the postal officials allowed me
to dispatch the package drastically understamped. Then there
followed a silence so total and long I forgot entirely about the
play. This did not displease me. I like throwing things into the
surrounding night and getting no reply at all. It is safer that
way.

A word came through at last. It was a guarded word, and
rather grudging. As far as I was concerned, the bloom seemed
to be off the novelists. Yes, they would give it a single, Sunday-
night performance to see if the thing would come to any sort of
reasonable life.

On the Sunday named I was driven to London by a friend. I
could not drive myself. Even in a bus, being driven, I develop
tensions that draw the eye of the driver and alienate my com-
panions. At the wheel and in command, my shouts of alarm
would scatter the public faster than a klaxon.

The journey seemed slow. I was moving through a thick
wool of unwillingness. We got to Northleach, on the road be-
tween Oxford and London, a minute after the pubs' opening
time. There were many pubs. We did the routine thing. We
went to them all, always looking for the one that would suggest
home, peace and eternity.

The sawdust bar of the first was full of men all with an iden-
tical oaken look about them. All were smiling. The first pints
of the day were slipping down like oysters. To have got in
and lifting ale so quickly they must have been waiting outside
and kicking the door on the stroke of twelve. They were as
broad as buses, just as placid, just as strong. If England does
not survive, ribbed by citizens like these, then something will
have gone gravely wrong with England's mind. One could not
expect behind any of those faces the malaise of imagining that
tricks most other communities into terror, self-mockery and
defeat. No goblins will ever find a gap in a collective psyche
composed of beer and a rooted sense of national identity. These
yeomen would not recognise the ultimate ruin of their tribe
even if the ruin were in front of them bowing patiently and
producing cards of identity from every pocket. Not even if the

final cards are delivered by nuclear blast.

The second pub we went into was a more thoughtful place. The landlord was an antiquarian, a man for whom the past needed to be tangible. He had come into possession of several pages from the log of the ancient Northleach gaol. They made a fascinating date. They belonged to the year 1808. One man goes to gaol for four months for removing a branch blown from a tree by a gale. The local lord laid claim to the tree and the gale and the gaol door opened. Another peasant charged with stealing a lamb is transported to Australia for eighteen years. In a place like the Cotswolds, manorial lords being poor with rope, hangmen were probably in short supply. A third entry spoke of a girl who was to be kept in Northleach gaol until she decided to reveal the identity of the father of her bastard child. She had, it was hinted, obdurately refused for a long while to do this. One could feel the embarrassed silences, the suspicious stares, the accusing glances centred around the cowering lass, more than probably imbecile, whose body had functioned with the warm openness of an inn for any lout with a penny to spare and a wish to sport his virility. The register was the usual curious mixture of arrogances and idiocies that one tends to find in most dealings between delinquents and their minders.

The handwriting had a grave, long-laboured loveliness. The most beautiful calligraphy would seem to be lavished on the ugliest facts: bank-ledgers, prison records. In letters of credit and letters de cachet every comma's tail must have its proper coat. Reading the pages I was as happily in the past as the landlord himself. Anything rather than think about that damned play.

Near the Lambert Arms, a splendid old coaching house at the foot of the hill that swept through woodland over to High Wycombe, we were nearly killed. Four drunken loons, standing up in their car. They were waving their arms, the driver included, and yelling like Liverpool football fans demented by sun, song and the heady culture of Scotland Road. These dervishes were on the wrong side of the road and coming into us at top speed. They had clearly pledged themselves over the lunchtime gin not to return home without having the boot of their car stuffed with the bodies of people coming innocently out of the West. We swerved on to the grass verge and through a hedge. We were badly shaken and the last thing I heard before being swung into the dark was the laughter of the revellers growing thicker and crazier. In the field on the other side of the hedge I lurched about for a while, seeking a chance to steal a sheep and get put away in the comparative safety of a convict settlement. There were no sheep. We returned to the road.

Just beyond High Wycombe the sky darkened in the fashion of a Bible story. At first we thought it might be a side-effect of our slight concussion. But our eyes were right. The sky was shedding its light hours ahead of dusk. My old hatred of London thickened with the gloom. I warmed my mind with thoughts of the great bucolic solitaries, anarchists, tree-lovers, herbalists, the Cobbetts and Thoreaus who laid their curse on conurbations.

'This darkness,' I said, 'unless it was sent by Moses to humble the English Stage Company and rupture the ghost of Shaw, is simply the shadow of the Great Wen, the evil town.'

My companions stroked my head to ease the pressure. The gloom explained itself. The clouds gave up and London had its heaviest deluge of rain since official records clocked their first shower. Every street became a river, with the water rising visibly. The car felt like a bathyscope and appeared now and then to be floating sideways. We peered out of the windows, looking for fish or Cousteau. Deciphering road-signs was no problem. The water took you right up to the message.

Somewhere near Hyde Park the rubber sheaths of our windscreen-wipers worked loose. One of them did the job properly and landed squarely on the hat of an ornately dressed woman. It settled without any sense of anomaly among the hat's other drenched decorations. We did not have the nerve to reclaim it. 'Excuse me, madam. My wiper.' Not in that sort of rain, anyway.

We stopped at Speakers' Corner where, in normal conditions, committed men violently hammer dialectical nails that vanished

from the average sight fifty years ago. One of our party tried to
wrench the surviving wiper, now halfway to freedom, back into
fixity. The upper half of the wiper's steel spine came away in
his hand. There were no speakers on Speakers' Corner. In flood
conditions free speech, as an issue, tends to recede. Dark forms,
which might have been dead or exhausted orators, floated past
us.

We had booked in at the Regent Palace, just off Piccadilly
Circus. It was then regarded as a hub of gaiety by provincials.
The vast basket lounge, in the days before they junked up the
décor with asymmetrical petrifacts, was for tens of thousands
their first whiff of the high world. Scotsmen, Lancastrians,
Welshmen, eager to unscramble the facts behind Soho, mad for
the rub of wickedness, the scorch of hell, demanding a cosmo-
politan airing for every facet of the libido, flocked there.

We moored the car in a side-street. This was in the early care-
less phase of the sixties, so there were no traffic wardens around
to tell you either to burn the car or back it down to the Devon
border. The great lounge of the Regent was packed. Half Lon-
don seemed to have been washed in by the downpour. Hun-
dreds were standing, baying for cake and tea. I addressed a
waitress who had the least understanding face I had ever seen.
We explained that we were residents and qualified for a table
even in the middle of that throng. She half listened, blinking
and crumpling her pinny with hands that were touching mad-
ness. We worked hard at simplifying the message. She spotted
two vagrants who were doing nothing but taking up two chairs,
keeping warm and dry and staring into space. We got their
table.

The waitress, through a high railing of reluctance, took our
order. At that moment I had no fancy for tea as a drink. I wanted
something more able to change my mental pitch. I needed a few
liveners if I was to face, in two hours' time, a parade of my
words and furtive people on a stage. I ordered a beer. The wait-
ress announced with a shaking joy that we were not in licensed
time. I explained again that we were residents and privileged.
If one had a bed in a licensed place one was entitled to a little

extra-curricular booze. I threw in every word I could think of connected with the serving of beer outside hours.

The waitress must have thought I was the manager's brother or from the police. In a daze, she brought the beer. We ordered several more. But each time she insisted on a certain ritual. We had to produce the key to the bedroom which she inspected and touched. Then we had to sign our names on some chit. We thought she would get tired of this routine. But no. For each gill delivered, the key, the name. Navvies never worked harder for their ale than we did in that lounge.

We left for Sloane Square. The rain had stopped but everyone in the streets still looked stunned by the force of it. The doors of the Royal Court Theatre were closed tight. On the steps a considerable group of people had gathered and most of the faces I saw were gloomy. Several raised their eyes compassionately, as if to say that this was the sort of thing that would happen to them and to me. I recognised several faces as belonging to people who have projected the image of Wales to the world: Clifford Evans, Donald Houston, Meredith Edwards and Madeleine Thomas, all wearing the worried look that belongs to the Welsh, the least confident and the least liked of the Celtic minorities in Britain.

George Devine made his appearance. He was wearing a turtle-necked sweater that hung away from his body. He looked like a fugitive from the Salvation Army Reclamation Corps which handles the more evasive type of derelict. This surprised me. I thought that any Sunday occasion called for a tidy suit. But it looked as if, for George, Sunday was good news still to come. A pipe hung low from his teeth which, even without the pipe, looked perpetually clenched. His white hair was all over the place.

He greeted me and mounted the steps. He assumed an air of benign majesty which soon crumbled. The theatre, he said, was flooded. The crowd, all conditioned by and for the theatre, gave a short groan, and addressed me with a cluck of sympathy. The lower levels of the auditorium were under water, sewage water, and while he had heard of extravaganzas like *Cinderella* being done on ice, he had never heard of a straight play being done on sewage. This was followed by some of the thinnest laughter ever heard in Sloane Square. On top of that, said George, Battersea Power Station was awash and there was no electricity. Short of an issue of municipal diving bells, periscopes and candles, the play would have to be postponed for a week. Anyone wanting his money back could go to the box office. Nobody went, which I took as a kind of success and I smiled my thanks at the crowd.

George took me to a small hut behind the theatre where the actors were still assembled, or huddled. For they looked as shattered as a group of men and a woman possibly could. They had rehearsed with fervour for five days and had reached a sharp battle-fitness. They liked the play and the play seemed to like them. They recalled some of the play's jokes. They did me good. I had forgotten them. To me, after all that time, it was just another Dead Sea Scroll! The sewage was a bonus. Now this: Battersea and its batteries dead and the Royal Court Theatre the new Atlantis. It was, I agreed, a plain, bloody nuisance.

We went to the pub next door, a place full of theatrical people, Chelsea pensioners in later Victorian costumes, and hot meat pasties. The bar was lit by candles and with big gestures and deep voices we laved our sorrow. I could not share the genuine grief of the actors. Their ardour and pride had been doused by dirty water. I could not match their sense of outrage. I felt no strangeness. I seek in every circumstance a bloom of absurdity and the bloom is delivered on the dot.

I was grateful for the candles. Shadows are good for distracting one from continuous talk. But at half past seven, at the very instant when, with drier luck, the curtain would have gone up, Battersea Power Station got dried out and the lights came back on. That meant I had to listen and in no time at all I was waist deep in an analysis by the actors of their parts and lines. Changing groups got hold of me and projected bits of the dialogue, wanting to know if they were giving the right shape to certain words and phrases. I was out of depth. My ancient silences tore right down the middle. Bats flew. I felt like a monk invited to address a conference of courtesans. Any actor who tried a line out on me I shook by the hand and told him that as I had heard it over the years, in dreams, I was hearing it now. They were the play made flesh.

We stayed in the pub until it closed. I was out of my depth, after the long day, the long journey. The beer was heady. The jargon of theatrical technique, the anxieties of people caught up in the most slippery activity, the most wantonly ungrateful calling this side of overt crime, were even headier.

One of the cast who had been confident of a great success had organised a party in her flat. We went there. It was a good party. There were seventeen types of cheese and two men who wanted to buy a piece of the play. At that moment, between the racket being made by the guests and the smell of the cheese, I was not sure what exactly they wanted a piece of. So no deal was made.

When we got back to the hotel the unwilling waitress was still there. By now she accepted our status as residents. There was no rigmarole with passwords, keys, signatures. She came back with our drinks in less than half an hour. During that interval I reacted to the tensions of the day and fell apart. I slipped into the most stupefying of silent glooms. The waitress looked at me in something near alarm, as if convinced that the dark trifle of the day was going to be topped off with the cherry of a dead visitor. She offered to lace my next ale with a shot of sal volatile. I told her that my life was in so dead a faint it was beyond the reach even of so potent a tonic as that.

'My play drowned,' I said.

She did not look at all surprised.

The following Sunday, George Devine tried again. I repeated the journey to London. We paused once more at Northleach. I was hoping that they might have come up with more leaves from that prison register which I would read as a gesture of solidarity with the luckless, and a totem against the fall of any fresh absurdity.

There were no mishaps. The day stayed dry and calm and kind. The play was seen. The actors sparkled. Some people laughed. It stayed at the Royal Court for two months and suggested a means of leaving teaching short of organising inlets for illegal immigration along the Glamorgan coast, an area badly lit and loosely patrolled, just right for slipping in dark strangers.

The whole theatre experience was refreshing. Without any wish to drum up trade I found myself telling people without any proper context or need, 'I've got a play running at the Royal Court.' Sometimes this was misunderstood. A Canadian to whom I announced the news said, 'The Royal Court, eh? Before the Queen. Say, kid, that'll do you the world of good. Those people don't bother to see many plays.'

The actors were delighted when the play was transferred to the Piccadilly Theatre. The Piccadilly is on the edge of Soho and shares its ambience of litter-bins and gloomy cafés. Looking at that part of London one feels it would be humane if the refuse wagons were authorised to remove human beings in strict proportion with the waste they produce. Rubbish over a certain total cancels out the value of the people who produce it.

The Piccadilly Theatre itself has the proportions of a major hangar and the gaiety of a chapel. There were predictions that it would last a year. I began to sniff at brochures that spoke of the sun and to stare at estate-agents' folders that showed pictures of houses with great gables with high walls and trees, and facilities for making TV films about badgers and night-jars on the side. But the prophets were wrong. The play ran in its new home for a month and was succeeded by a play that ran for less. Changes of cast and the largeness of the theatre helped it into its coffin. As with sex and, they tell me, onion-growing, a transfer from a small and intimate place to a big and impersonal one rarely helps. I felt that I had satisfied any curiosity I might have felt about being a playwright.

*

George Devine was keen on a second play. He had two sug-

gestions along which he invited me to work. He explained the
ideas to me over long lunches. George in restaurants was worth
watching. He had a way of turning his head violently around
and crying, 'Maître d'hôtel!' in his strange, hollow, carrying
voice. I could never see anything wrong with the meal to justify
this outburst. It may simply have been that he liked the sound
of 'Maître d'hôtel' and his way of expressing it. It struck me as
a gesture of tone and potency and I told him he was free to
indulge it any time he fancied.

His ideas did not please me as much. The first was that I
should exploit my peck of Spanish scholarship and translate a
series of classics from the Spanish Golden Age. I did not re-
spond. The plays of that period rest on three main preoccupa-
tions. Theological obsession, miracles and kings of high intelli-
gence and tireless compassion, who intervene with splendid
justice in the affairs of their subjects. With the first theme I was
in touch. I had grown up through a life that had flared with
inflamed theologians who had lost light and point with every
day I subsequently lived. But the theology of the Spanish drama
was Catholic and I had little patience with any dogma that has
left a trail of bitter ash behind it. The main religious organisa-
tion of Spain has always caused me unease. Any institution that
ordains celibacy for its officials and demands rapid-fire breed-
ing from its sectaries, will always strike me as odd.

As for the other great themes of Spain's great century
miracles, and monarchs tireless in the cause of justice and the
defence of the meek, I have seen and heard nothing of either.
All good, inherited prejudice. But I think it no more than
courtesy to give the people who brain-washed me some return
on their soap. So I told George Devine that he could keep
Spain's Golden Age.

Then George said I should write a play of swinging social
protest. While the material of my early work had been the suc-
culent proletarian mouthful of the Rhondda Valley, I had
scarcely touched any of the scabrous and sensational elements in
the lives of those I wrote about. I saw much radiance and good-
ness, a brightness of tongue and heart, an almost witless

idealism. It was these things that held my eye and drove my pen, the whole great jumping joke of so many men and women, highly literate, wedded in equal measure to religious devotion and political militancy, invoking the mercy of God and the wisdom of Lenin in a worsening world.

I suppose this addiction to presenting the case for the hopeful, the decent and articulate among the unprivileged made me, in the strictly professional sense, the biggest sucker of my time. If someone could have strengthened my nerve of malignancy, sent me bright-eyed to prowling around the stews and fetched me back with a bulging bagful of incest, illiteracy, lice, kitchen abortions, casual and loveless adulteries, the whole armoury of squalor, I suppose I could have really hit the till at some point or another. But I did not and feel no sense of having behaved wrongly. To describe in detail the antics of the degraded is, in an odd way, to lengthen the lease of the degraded. The debased and foul are, in the main, the casualties of stupid government as road-crash victims are the casualties of stupid driving.

I still feel a sense of horror as I read the works of novelists from the decayed areas of the North and Midlands, swarming out of their side-alleys and backyards, dragging their tin tubs loaded to the brim with the muck of every known type of defilement. Write as many theses on caries as you will, the human mouth remains a fairly good proposition.

So I said no to the notion of a contemporary play of social protest. I was out of touch. Not quite as far as Noël Coward, but edging that way. The people for whom I had wished to speak had long since shut up. They had seen their dreams turn swiftly to mud. Their waving banners had gone up in flames or hardened in frost. The broad, hymnal hopes that had sprouted from a gross oppression had been replaced by the invincible idiocy of those being emancipated by the piecemeal reform of fussy first-aiders. Rush to heed the cries for help of a damsel or a whole social class in distress and, as often as not, you will be let down disastrously by the appearance, mind and idiom of those to whose assistance you have gone. All perilous nonsense, of course, but for a man with hardening cells in mind and heart,

K

pleasant nonsense which is hard to come by.

On top of that, I had had my fill of the grunting cretins who had come surfacing up in so many post-war plays. The mad, the mannerless and the lousy operate, for me, on a shortening rope of charm. And the brave new themes of rape and buggery, for all my interest in broadening the scope of human hobbies, did not engage my mind.

And yet I felt the need to do something that would theatrically excite. If ever you want a recipe for failure, that is it. There is no darkness so impenetrable as that between a proposed play and its intended audience. Whole diseases of change fall upon the writer and the listener at a minimum rate of once a week.

What I eventually did arose from what Marie Curie called the energy of despair. That, and about ten thousand red vitamin pills which I had been told had been known to resurrect cordial urges dead for a decade or more. The only urge I was interested in was literary. I would not waste a penny of pill money on any other. After years of writing rather quiet philosophic novels featuring no weapon deadlier than the blunter type of chip-shop fork, I had a fancy to write something gusty and rollicking, festooned with horses, gibbets and mayhem in all its stock sizes. It was rather like the impulse that drives sober actuaries to read *Treasure Island* every week-end. There was some inward chill that had to be challenged and driven off. I wanted tables bandy-legged beneath a load of silver, bosses bent double beneath the weight of brocade. I got two undertakers to screw down my old concern with the contemporary toiler. The chip-shop was way, way behind.

The transition was a natural one. A life-long addiction to grand opera and the mindless melodrama of the cinema made it inevitable that one day I would move away from wry chronicles of the brighter among our *sans-culottes*. In a social ambience so emphatically tainted by lunacy as that of a mining area moving into dereliction, I took even the dottiest libretto in my stride and would have accepted Tarzan the Apeman as a normal type of councillor. Short on serge and agenda, but a good democratic representative in the making, just right for quick movement up and down walls in our more ivied slums.

The plots of the early and middle Verdi, in which probability stands in the middle of the stage shocked and gaping, I accepted as prosaic reality and were given regular amateur performance in our town. I found no difficulty in accepting that a vengeful gypsy, whose mother has been burned at the stake by a duke, should not only wish to burn the duke's child but actually burn her own child in error. Our feeling about dukes was so intense it would have led us, too, to fumble the big occasion. A predilection for violence, ashes and terrible errors overlay my entire culture. From the age of seven I was, emotionally, eye-deep in volcanic coke.

Years later, when I was the tutor of a cultural group in an Educational Settlement, we were pursuing a course called The European Mind, which covered everything from the amoeba to the burning tip at Bedlinog, a well-known local nuisance except to the chillier type of voter who wants to be set alight by the floating embers.

One evening we got on to the subject of Verdi's *Force of Destiny*, an opera in which coincidences go off like cosmic gongs. For my ear, aware of dislocation as a major idiom, they had a rational rhythm. I gave the group an analysis of this work so excessively cogent it still has some of them confused and looking at me as if I were Luno, their brother from the moon. The play is an epic of revenge, and seeing the world at that time as a pretty malignant parish, I had cordial feelings about revenge and I could treat with Don Alvaro (a descendant of the last Inca, a masochist and unlucky with firearms) and the sons of the Marquis of Calatrava (he is accidentally shot dead in the middle of Don Alvaro's attempt to elope with his daughter), as fellow lodge-members. As for the helpless heroine, Leonore, living as a hermit in that solitary grotto near a monastery in the high sierra, a total anathema promised to any monk who might dare to air his tonsure in the vicinity, I knew dozens of female neighbours who, psychologically, were doing just that without even the consolation of having arrived at their impasse through a violent pattern of caste-snobbery and mayhem.

At about the same period I did service as an unpaid stage manager to a company that was frightening the wits out of audiences in the local Welfare Hall with performances of such works as *The Dumb Man from Manchester* and *The Crimes of Stephen Hawkes*. Hawkes was a man who had the strength to break people's backs as others do matchsticks, and for motives varying from greed to simple pleasure, he used it. One of Hawkes' ways of keeping his strength up and signalling his next crime was to crack the joints of his knuckles. I, off stage, had to simulate this noise because the actor concerned was useless with knuckles.

And, of course, Sweeny Todd, the murderous barber who used his customers as a filling for pies. To this theme I sensed no reaction of horror in the audience. They had seen so much of governments which, with larger resources than Todd, still managed to keep half the species famished, there was an almost articulate wish to back the barber for some election or another.

Besides stage management and seeing that the barber's chair really tilted the slain clients into the pie factory, I also appeared as a passing stranger who peers through the window, a kind of omen of the doom that was surely on the way, and as doom was constantly on the way in the plays we performed, I was always somewhere near the window, leering. The producer, a sucker for omens, liked this effect. He even had me enlarge the window so that the audience could get the full flavour of what, in those days, was a savagely saturnine and disturbing face.

It was, I suppose, all part of a general campaign to bury subtlety which can always be regarded as an anti-democratic ploy. I had offers from two local landlords to beam a few of my fierce glares on to tenants whose connection with the cash nexus had become hopelessly slack. From those appearances people came so to regard me as a headlamp of approaching calamity that for years after whenever they spotted me they would hide or dust their death policies.

So, with that background, it was inevitable that I should edge my way back to melodrama as a thermal dodge to ease me through my autumn. But melodrama invested with a kind of verbal dignity denied to those plain-spoken monomaniacs, Todd and Hawkes. And a range of ideas that would have stood Todd, the demon barber, on his ear and rushing for the brush to stop my mouth.

With these memories trailing me around I started casting about for the theme that later became *Jackie the Jumper*. You will not have heard of it. In a period of constantly leaking security in Britain this play was one of the few secrets utterly well kept. It passed through its phase of public life with the darkling modesty of a liver-fluke.

I considered the possibility of a Spanish theme, thinking that George Devine's instructive compass might have flickered well. There was also the old early Verdi trauma and the baked-gypsy motif still kicking around for laughs. I gave a thought to the revolt of the Comuneros in 1520, an incident in which Carlos Quinto suppressed insurrection and did a brisk undertaking job on Spanish democracy for centuries to come, and left the cadaver of a stifled radical on every tree from Cadiz to Segovia. This name still glitters through the night of the years and suggests what would have happened to us if Cromwell had failed, as the weavers of Segovia failed in their fight for burghers' rights.

Now and then the imbeciles actually do win and that is an awful thought. What would have eventuated in America had George III and his attendant dolts had their way over Washington and Jefferson? It was, by the way, one of those Segovian weavers who sent a gift of silk stockings to a Spanish queen and was beheaded for daring to suggest that a Spanish queen had legs. Without royal courts humanity would have been grossly short on clowns.

But my mind came back to the place where it abidingly belongs: South Wales. I wanted a play that would paint the true face of sensuality, rebellion and religious revivalism; roaring debauch, intemperate petulance and whimpering hangover. In South Wales these three phenomena have played second fiddle only to hernia viewed as a way of life, bandy-legs stemming from lack of protein and a compelling urge to walk with a kind of lecherous strut, sex viewed as an aspect of gunmanship, and the Rugby Union which is a distillation of the lot, brutal Old Testament ferocity tempered by the curious Greek moods of men crowded together in a steaming post-match bath and a night of beer-logged piety.

I wanted a theme that would illustrate the curious seesaw of passivity and defiance in human life. To ask why some stir it up and others allow the scum of conformity and defeat to form into a mortal pall above their heads. The urge to exult and love at odds with the compulsive wish to geld and part.

My growing-up place, the dark, octopal gulches I never wished to leave, whose embrace, whenever it grew slack, I would stroke back into a pitiless rigidity, was the classic arena of this duel. Political turbulence and a fiercely flowering libido singed the minds and the fern-beds of the zone. As children prowling the hillsides, we often took the prone mass of copulants and the moving forms of ageing voyeurs to be part of the flora.

Time and again one would have the feeling that disgust and love had reached a climactic tumescence that would have life bursting its breeches in no time at all, and no money to spare for a replacement. Preachers of an operatic force and brilliance: harmonised hymns of a plangency to wash away all the rocks of grief and the grimaces of thought. Between a chill humidity, raging rhetoric and tireless singing, this is a nation with a very sore throat.

Often, leaving the chapel after an interminable sermon and six rousing hymns in a building left gaunt and hollow to make an awesome sound-box for every vocal register, one would have an ache for sensual relief in some shape or form that would have bleached our elders' bowlers if they had truly known how perverse are the tides of piety in the minds of the younger sectaries. But they had us firmly held in their loved and heavy chains. We must never fall below the level of their revelations, sunlit by the word of God and kept spinning by their own athletic terrors.

Our night was full of their hurt, bewildered eyes. All delights of sight or touch were to be shunned as part of the world's fallible and fissile truss of fleshly comforts. We had had the golden assurance of an everlasting non-human love. If, on the way downwards from the Sunday storm-cloud we dared wink back at the ancient obscenity of the ape, it we fondled the fabric of our clothes or the stones of a flanking wall or the condensed water on the wrought-iron railings of the collapsed and crooked graveyard through which ran a deep and terrible fault, disquieting the dead, we were charged with a brazen carnality. For children, the odds in the whole game of breathing were inscrutable.

Then, in answer to every wave of libertarian fumbling, would come a wind of evangelism, a hot sirocco that had the whole population cowering, sweating or buttoning up, depending on their primal relations with heat. And I, magnetised by both factions, jumped like a grasshopper, back and fore between the charms of sin and that of redemption. Whether the cause was earthly insurrection or heavenly salvation, I was always one of the leading banner-bearers. I just believed in banners and expressing a loud, public identity. My bardic name was ambivalence. Even now, twice a day, I change my trousers from back to front, just to play it safe.

So, the facts I chose for Jackie the Jumper were loosely gathered from the early Chartist movement. The Merthyr Riots of 1831, to be exact. The land had known a drop in the price of metal and a rise in the price of bread. You may rely on any government, coming across two facts of that sort, to slap them sharply together and make them worse. The local Jacobins, choked by the pest-holes in which they puddled their iron and the demands of their hungry wives and infants, began to feel that the people in command were an uppity set of bastards who wanted their teeth shaking.

They were not quite right. They did not realise that economic facts, regardless of class, have an independent and seemingly imbecile life of their own. Many of the iron-masters were men of great resource. One of them, known for his ruthless impar-

tiality, sold weapons to both sides during Washington's War of
Liberation. A later one loved Verdi and subsidised brass bands.
But try explaining these things to a man whose stomach is
rumbling and who is staving off the approach of bailiffs. You
have to shout a bit.

The people lose in a brief and futile bout of temper. A few
fell before the muskets of the County Militia, a crew of storm-
troopers who switched from fox-hunting to man-killing with
no sense of strain at all. The rising was led by two men called
Dic Penderyn and Lewis the Huntsman. Dic was an iron-
worker, a family man, Lewis was a libertarian vagabond. They
were captured and tried in Cardiff by a rabidly biassed judge and
jury. Dic was hanged. Lewis, said by legend to be the son of a
lovely and high-born lady, survived and went to America. His
vagabondage not only did not cease but broadened. He drifted
back to this country more than once. People claimed that they
saw him, a gaunt figure, staring down from the hillside at the
foot of which Dic lay buried. Jackie the Jumper is an amalgam
of those two men but I did not have the time or wish to make
this clear, so a lot of people never got the point.

The Dic Penderyn character had been long in my mind. I
could not have been more than seven when the name and the
fact of him arrived to stay. I was walking with my father over
the mountain to a pub where by some bit of guile or influence
he was able to get a drink on Sunday. Suddenly he pointed
dramatically at the great ridge to the north-west, the high moor-
land that separated the Rhondda from the Afan Valley.

'That was where they took him,' he said.

'Took who?'

'Dic Penderyn, the martyr. Long time ago now. Fiery and
bold. Accused after the Merthyr Riots of setting fire to a bake-
house and molesting some militiaman. Lies, all lies, I suppose.
I'd never trust any story told by a baker or a militiaman. A false
lot. He was tried by a harsh judge, a defender of privilege and
fanatically down on rioters and doctrines of dissent. He
wouldn't have thought less if the inside of his head had been
stuffed by his own wig. They hanged him at Cardiff. His wife

and two children were standing right there in front of the scaffold. They did these things in public in those days. To give the masses the full flavour, see what I mean. They put his body on a farm-cart and brought him up this valley, over the ridge and down into the next valley. A great time for grief and singing. From every cleft of the hillside came groups to march and mourn and sing behind Dic in the cart. Look hard at the ridge. You should see them, for a death that draws the tears of many people you never even knew has a special taste and never vanishes from the earth. Can you see them? Dic, the cart, the singing people?'

'No.'

'You will. Your sight will improve as your heart grows. They took him all the way down the next valley. It must have been a slow journey, for if there's one thing we like it is to drag out a funeral. Just as well the dead don't notice. His grave is in Aberavon and, true to form, no one gives a damn about it.'

I made my first large novel from this idea. I say large because my first few novels were small affairs, written during the war on some brand of yellow paper that soaked in the ink and made it virtually invisible. They reflected the stupid terrors of the time. Published later they might have won me a fair bit of cash and credit. They contained a heavy ration of unnatural sex (man on high-level protein diet commits incest with three daughters), existentialist slayings (boy, in dark, leads horseman and horse over a quarry because he wants to know what sound the impact will make), and metallic cynicism honed to race-gang standard. By the time I could afford something better than that yellow paper my mood had become calm and philosophic, and almost mortally non-titillant.

I was glad with Jackie the Jumper to give the Merthyr Riots another run for their skeletal money, and to project, through the Jumper himself, a brand of sexiness that would have my elder brothers and sisters, puritans to a man, leaving the theatre flanked and supported by ushers.

In Britain we have had extraordinarily few riots. A deep stream of ale to dilute most rages and free outlets of disputation among the plebs, and a full seam of self-protective cunning among the patricians have kept our social body jogging along without too many civil commotions. So we tend to cherish the ones we've had, carry them around as proudly as a Tahitian would his necklace of sharks' teeth.

Involved in that ancient patch of violence is Jackie the Jumper, philosophic anarchist and sexual Olympian, shuttling between long stints at the foundries and fornication, smelting and deflowering to the mad rhythm of a mad time. Facing him is his uncle, Richie 'Resurrection' Rees, a thundering divine. And between them the early struggles of a society tormented and besmirched by the eruption of the great iron furnaces and the descent of the great Calvinistic vetoes. Dionysus beating the living lights out of St Paul and the other way about.

Indeed, the play opened with a dozen pairs of lovers poised for some mass coupling. Their spirits have been raised to a lascivious peak by the prospect of an imminent strike. Had they been allowed to carry this tableau to full realisation I could have been in the chips if the Lord Chamberlain could have been fobbed off with a chip of his very own. On the second day of the run there began a series of blizzards unique in the records of foul weather. Plays died like flies and mine got to the boneyard first.

*

I was to have a third bite of the theatrical apple and my teeth went into action quite by accident. I was sitting in the staffroom of my school during the mid-morning tea-break. The room was packed. Its floor was uncarpeted, footsteps loud. Teachers in private session tend to be garrulous and even those who do not talk manage to make a lot of sound. With despair working towards a full head of steam they can make a sigh go off like a sniper's rifle.

The telephone rang. The thing was inside the room and was rarely answered. The news it diffused was seldom important: football fixtures made or cancelled, domestic mishap in the

home of a staff-member or some boy who, for one or five
reasons, had locked himself in the toilet. There was one col-
league, a timid and suggestible man, who could be persuaded,
against his will, to pick up the receiver and read the signals. As
the phone bell rang we would all stare at him and raise our eye-
brows. He would rise with them and would proceed like a
zombie to the telephone. He had received many gloomy mes-
sages in the past, two fires and two attacks on his aunt, a vulner-
able postmistress in a criminous patch of the town, and we had
lain upon him a spell of conviction that this was another one.
He stood poised to give his head a grave shake as another piece
of sky landed on it.

He listened nervously and told me the call was for me.
Against the odds, I got up to answer it. The phone was lodged
on a shelf, inside an arch of perforated wood that was supposed
to make the caller crystal clear. They must have used the wrong
sort of perforations or the endless piles of books on either side
of the arch sucked in the sound, or the racket of teachers in a
bout of long-relaxed banter built up a resistance to Bell. The
reception was terrible. On top of that I am a telephobe. I dis-
trust and rarely comprehend any sound that comes to me via
wires. As soon as a receiver touches my ear I contract a kind of
nervous deafness. Muffling curtains fall from every corner of
my skull. As a user of modern media Marshall MacLuhan
would not give me house-room. My last chance as a technocratic
activist went out with the making of witches' brooms.

I scrootched my head and shoulders into the arch and listened
with dedication. I realised that I had been too flippant in my
view and treatment of our contemporary miracles and was
determined to do better and shed a large slice of my defensive
idiocy.

The voice on the other end was high, hurried and aristo-
cratic. I caught his name: Richard Rhys. He sounded amiable
and I was sorry that his name was the only thing that emerged
without ambiguity from what he said. I apologised for my lack
of ability as a phoner and told him that the school was in the
middle of a fire drill and that I was at that moment holding, in

addition to the phone, two water buckets and a nozzle and a memorandum on what to do for boys who jumped out of windows rather than listen to the cool wisdom of the school's fire marshals. These footnotes did less than nothing to help the mental action along. I asked him to call me back at home where communication had an easier time of it.

I went from the phone and sat down alongside a colleague, Mr Hare, with whom normally I had nothing to do. He was a tireless snob. He read the gossip columns of every paper he could get his hands on. He had committed to heart the genealogy of every nationally famous family in Britain. Once when threatened by anaemia he refused a course of liver extract and, instead, touched a copy of *Burke's Peerage*, a thick book which is mainly about blood and its lines of influence. He was cured and has spent most of his time since praising Burke and running down liver.

On general social grounds Mr Hare regarded me as a wrong one and shunned me. But lately he had tolerated me because I had been invited, for my services to literacy, to a Royal Garden Party held in the locality. Mr Hare had been disappointed by the coverage I brought back from this function, and he made it plain he thought I had spent the afternoon skulking in the beer-tent in a fit of republican sulks. But Mr Hare was wrong. That Garden Party, the sort of event my instincts should have clearly warned me to avoid, was an occasion when little had gone right for me. I had missed seeing the Queen pass, being held up looking for a toilet in a maze of privet hedges. The one-time owner of the estate where the rally took place had been a coal-owner and a sadist with a fancy for setting down comfort-stations in the middle of labyrinths, plying his guests at open-air fêtes with diuretic fluids like cider, and then watching them emerge from their wanderings hopping with strain and bursting with chlorophyl.

He would have enjoyed me. I almost ruptured a vein and missed the Queen as well. I also had my hat blown off and was prevented from chasing it by a platoon of sullen ushers who thought I was a terrorist.

Three things helped me to keep my balance. Numerous friends of mine were there whom I failed to recognise at first sight because they were rigged out in some of the most antique looking bits of hired finery I have ever seen. Pendulous tails from sagging coats made clear tracks in the first fall of autumn leaves as their wearers progressed across the turf. Hats of excessive height on the loftier Celts seemed to be bringing on rain. Many carried their hats and tried to look as if they had just found them and wished to return them to someone.

Two long lines of women, arranged in the middle of the grounds to provide an avenue of obeisance for the Queen, ran into some mild trouble. It had rained heavily during the three previous weeks. The women all wore shoes with heels of a baroque height. As they stood motionless to welcome the royal presence they could be seen getting shorter. At first I thought it signified some form of inert reverence special to people who are getting over a long period of restrictive republicanism. It was the women's heels sinking into the sodden loam. They stayed anchored there, squat, immobile and shamed until the Queen had passed, and many a husband did himself an injury levering and rocking them free of the clay. The brass band lost a lot of their sheet music when some gust of wind that did for my hat bowled over half their music stands.

The Duke of Edinburgh and myself were in lounge suits and stayed outside the flunkey belt. I spotted at least four men in suits of undue splendour, put out of countenance by the Duke's informality, hiding behind privet hedges. That was my first and only run as a courtier. On drier ground and a calmer day I might have done better, but I do not think so. For the thousandth time I had the strong sense of being a bee, buzzing with willingness but outside the wrong hive and stung by my leader for being laden with the wrong pollen.

When Mr Hare first heard me describe the details of that afternoon and causing amusement among the looser egalitarians, he had tightened the strings of his face to create a more resonant contempt and his eyes grew cold. He gave me a glance that I might have expected from Metternich or Viscount

Chaplin, a politician of the late Victorian time whose prejudices in favour of inherited customs were of teak.

But Mr Hare had not been able to rid himself of the feeling that you could never treat as wholly an exile one who had been invited by the Queen to something other than a war. That won a man at least one spur. And since Mr Hare regarded me as socially one-legged, that was enough. He still thought that my conduct on that royal afternoon had been of an unseemliness which would have cost me my head in a more reverent age. He had told me that any man who, at the climax of such an event, the Queen's actual proximity, could find himself chundering about in a maze looking for a urinal should be examined and put down. Royal people managed these things better. Used to hours of long and unrelieved pomp, they had in this particular developed powers of endurance that would have baffled a Water-Board. And in the same connection he had told me a story about George V at some ceremony in New York of which I did not get the point, but the incident seemed to have impressed Grover Whalen and Mayor Walker, the last a man impatient under pressure.

Mr Hare gave a half-smile as I sat down at his side after the telephone message.

'Mr Hare,' I said, 'the gentleman who just called me had a high, hurried, aristocratic mode of speech. His name is Richard Rhys. Between his style of address and the unsocial structure of my inner ear I did not catch more than a fragment of what he said. Who is Richard Rhys?'

The name registered at once. Mr Hare showed excited interest and the facts flowed like wine. Mr Hare's mind, in its traffic with the *haut monde*, was automated. Richard Rhys was the son and heir of the Lord Dynevor, one of the oldest families in Wales. They had a gracious estate and castle near Llandeilo. Mr Hare had once been there on a coach outing, one of a servile delegation meant to reassure titled land-owners of popular support. Mr Hare was aware of having been served a very strong drink by a butler in the early evening and of having seen a large herd of deer on the edge of the woodland facing the

front of the castle. Mr Hare drank little, and the deer could
have been a mild delirium.

'The Welsh aristocracy at its best,' he said, and he made it
clear that he thought this call from Richard Rhys was not far
behind the summons to the Royal Garden Party in significance.
'Do you realise that if by some happy quirk of time and chance,
if Britain should collapse, as well it might, into ruined pieces
and Wales reverted to its ancient monarchical impulses,
Richard Rhys could well be the first king of a new united Wales.
And what did Dynevor's heir want with you?'

'Something to do with writing a play.'

'Oh.' He was disappointed. He would have been better
pleased if the Dynevors had suggested I become herdsman of
their ancestral stags. 'I think the old families should keep away
from things like that. Very cheapening, the theatre. The noble
families should avoid anything that exposes them to obloquy
or tempts them into vulgarity. With the rest of society liques-
cing into mud, a dry and frigid dignity is their only viable tic-
ket.' He looked and sounded like Herald Garter, Black Rod or
some other caparisoned cog of the Establishment.

'Suppose so,' I said, making a note to ask Hare, before his
day of retirement, to let me have some samples of his brain tissue
for submission to the St Fagan's Folk Museum, the one-time
home of the Earl of Plymouth, where the quainter aspects of
Welsh life are on view to the public.

When I got home Richard Rhys phoned again. We arranged
to meet for a conference at an hotel in Cardiff called the Big
Windsor. It was a dockside pub, beautifully shaped, with an
arrogantly dirty exterior and a good kitchen. It was popular
with stage and television people. The bar through which one
passed to get to the restaurant had overtones of the Barbary
Coast, and the customers drank their pints as if washing down
a quartered revenue man.

Richard Rhys was a tall, stooped and gracious man. His sur-
face was shy and diffident and it still surprises me to think that
before our dealings were done he would prove himself to be as
obdurate as an ascending Mafia captain.

He ordered coq au vin, the boast of the house, for both of us. With a few tremors of chapel reluctance against the idea of eating drunken fowl, I did my best to enjoy the meal, concentrating on the chips and trying not to be put off by Richard's intense enthusiasm.

He had, he said, a great idea for a musical. He was speaking more quickly now than he had on the phone. His eyes were bright and his whole tall being was charged with a euphoria striking against so gloomy a background as Cardiff's dockland. I took it as stemming from some obstinate vitality in the enclosed, pure-blooded stock to which he belonged. The survival of aristocracy argues either some supernormal flair in the aristocrats or some abysmal infirmity in those towards whom they stand in the aristocratic relationship. Probably the latter, since the infirmity of victims is as enjoyable and infinitely less taxing than the ruthless activity of predation.

His look saddened for an instant when he saw that my enthusiasm did not match his. My attention was not altogether on him. One part of my senses was trying to figure out what wine they had added to my chicken. Another was trying to listen to a waitress at the next table. She was a kindly, large, heavy woman. She was explaining to a pair of customers that she and two of her colleagues, all three of them well lodged in middle age, had been taught to do the Can-Can, a tempestuous, knicker-revealing jig, by the actor Hugh Griffiths. Hugh, in the mood of expansive diabolism that matches his eyes and will, had gone to this task with passionate zeal. The ladies would not have been more galvanised had Toulouse-Lautrec, that dark jewel in Paris's golden age of whoredom, been calling the shots. It had, said the waitress, given them all new life and when they hit top form between the heat of the rhythm and the weight of feet made leaden by a million journeys from kitchen to table, they could just about shake the place apart. A rite of telling exposures and flying soup.

One night, not long before, the oldest of the three had volunteered to do the dance on a table-top. A late and drunken diner, seeing legs cavorting at eye-level just ahead of him, thought this was a tassel dangling from some new delirium, foreswore liquid and pushed his soup away. The dancing waitress, bewitched by Hugh's satanic glare, had misjudged the size of the table and gone crashing to the floor and injured an arm.

'A marvellous idea for a musical,' said Richard.

My mind did not hasten to make contact. I kept listening to the waitress with her warm evocation of the demi-monde, the twilight of smiling lubricity that vanished and left us wondering, through the war-burned and tax-bitten years, if Hubert Humphrey and Patrick Gordon Walker are any kind of fair return for Cora Pearl and La Belle Otero.

On top of these distractions the mention of musicals fills me with a kind of terror. I have never failed to find them one of the dreariest dodges in a fairly dehydrated epoch. And at that time the phrase 'Listen to this as an idea for a musical' had become almost as familiar a form of greeting as axioms about the weather. I knew a man who had played about with the idea of basing a musical on a Government White Paper on effluent in the Bristol Channel, with singing parts for complaining fish and chosen bits of waste. But he gave up when he became interested in effluent for its own sake and he took to spending his week-ends patrolling beaches warning people about pollution, thickening the threads of concern and being largely misunderstood for his trouble. Another man thought he saw the makings of a bonanza musical in the Book of Job if he could play down the boils motif and step up the love interest.

'What's it about, this musical?'

He explained. The central figure is a bullying pimp in a club in Bute Street, Cardiff. This street is the long, gaunt main avenue of Cardiff's dock area. Once it was the lair of a posse of uniquely gifted, greedy and ruthless privateers who climbed on to a throne of astonishing power during the years when the Welsh coal-ports reached the top of the world's commercial charts. The streets around their Exchanges were known, for their brawls and knifings, as Tiger Bay. The tiger has moulted long since. The only frisson now yielded by the place is that felt by minds to which a coloured skin is sinister.

L

The rough-tongued tyrants who, by their indifference to reasonable marine-safety standards, drowned almost as many seamen as the German Fleet, are scarcely remembered, except by ageing minions who recall, against a background of pinching shabbiness, the five-pound tips of drunken tycoons after a champagne and kippers breakfast in one of the mansions where they luxuriated in blood-stock, bad grammar and insanely easy profits. The tamed Bay is as quiet as moss. Tedium demolishes lives as the bulldozers flatten the houses.

Little remains of yesterday's tainted triumphs outside the opulent Stock Exchange, silent now but for the giggling ghost of some speculator celebrating his wise and timely death. Inside the Exchange the furnishings include specimens of timber from every corner of the Empire over which it now stands as one of many modest gravestones. Children's scrawls in whitewashed alleys of what look like Damascan skylines remind one of the thousands of Arab families that flowed freely into this area in the days before our immigration policy froze at the edges as it did in America forty years before.

It was a place I disliked. I have never had a grain of patience with areas that men have fouled and been too slow to clean up or remove. Very few men of commercial genius have passed through this life without leaving a broadening wake of appalling dinginess. From now on they should be given a big brush to tidy up before they are given their barony. Also, in the Bute Street enclave, the mind is constantly invaded by the fug that attends any aspect of race difference, race-hatred. Men know that most of their number suffer from basic intellectual defects, lack of mental audacity, failure of taste, and they seek always for monomanias that will excuse them from the torments of continuous thought, will give them the chance to be officially and delightedly stupid. Chauvinism, sex and race are the dark trinity that head the curriculum of the idiot. You will find traces of all three in Tiger Bay.

No white-skinned dullard can pass through it without being braced by the oxygen he senses in the presence of people he thinks of as inferior and sub-articulate. To sensitive and censorious ears a loud-voiced harlotry rises from dusk onwards, and coitus, in the dockside tenements, is regarded as being as loud and persistent as hymn-singing in the valleys to the north. Withered little Caucasians in their leather-chaired clubs, whisper of elegantly dressed and wealthy white women queueing at Dockland doors for the favours of lucky and monstrously endowed Jamaicans, Ghanaians or whatever.

This litany is as well-worn as the Decalogue and just as futile. It scares the eyeballs off me. I would have said that Tiger Bay was as suitable to me as material for a play as the interior of Buckingham Palace or the public confidences of a politician.

I should have said this directly to Richard. I should have made it flatly plain that there was no theme in the place where we sat which would not strike me as infertile and repellent to the last degree. I should not have allowed wine-soaked chicken and a fine line in chips to come between me and frankness. But plain speaking has never been my art and could well be my death, and it is only those whose obliquity could cause a nation's ruin and a world's decay would never make a confession of that sort. If truth were a disease I would not have been in a greater hurry to be immunised. So, I listened to Richard, cautiously but without protest.

The musical would be violent. The bullying pimp, a Maltese club-owner, will be a smart hand with a knife. His rival is a boxer and guitarist who, I took it, also wanted to carve out something in the pimp-stakes. Stabbing, boxing and guitar provide fine balletic growing points. Look at *West Side Story*. But I got the point. I had done a long solitary post-midnight walk in New York and had imagined in every doorway and alley the glinting shivs of lurking muggers.

The bullying pimp fixes boxing bouts and promotes whores. His club is thronged with girls from the Afro-Arabian quarter, deep-voiced, self-defensively insolent, diluted by girls who have drifted down from the mining places, unable to endure one more gulp of the gruesome cocktail of coal and Calvin. The club swings between the poles of lechery and sport. Even the copulation is tempered by the simpler rules of Queensberry. As far as I could tell Queensberry's son, Lord Alfred Douglas, failed to get past the doorman, which I thought was weakening the script in advance.

'All right. I'll tackle it. A club, pimps, knives, boxing, miscegenation, whoredom as an aspect of demography. If nymphomania were laid on in the tap-water, lust would drift a lot less. Sounds a rich mixture.'

Against the background of my first thoughts about this venture I stopped eating and settled down to some soberly sociological thought about the chronic battlefields of human disunity. Then the waitresses started the Can-Can, ineptly done but, up against sociology, a nice change.

I went to work on the play. My pen-hand had never moved more warily to a task. I had written about squalor before, but not this kind, not voluntary squalor, half-enjoyed by the people involved, who saw in degradation a sort of macabre joy, who found in what the people of my growing-up time would have considered shame, something as toothsome as caviar, something as bracing and satisfying as the thing fox-hunters find in hunting and hurting foxes, the immortal and immutable jokers of the human pack.

I decided to play the thing as a guttering of the Victorian ethic. This would make the work the millionth try in this line of surgery. A few avant-garde pathologists claim, on the basis of a few skirts that have put the navel in the middle of the shop-window, that repression as a social idiom is as dead as the stone it so much resembled. I do not think so. Try sliding on any slippery slope of gaiety in Britain and you will be surprised how quickly you get your pants torn on small glaciers of pre-1914 censoriousness. As I drafted the book for Richard's musical I looked for images and events that would check and chasten the frigid nuisances who still go poking and choking around at the suspicion of any irreverence.

So I assembled the materials of some simple-witted slapstick which might cause some defensive hopping among the Aunt Sallies who believe in further separating in terms of nationalism, sex, wealth, colour, an already lonely and distracted pack of human beings. My first move was to make the bullying pimp stop being a Maltese and give him a British origin and name. I did not want to add any loose libels to an already insecure national minority. Also, during the war, Malta won a decoration called the George Cross for holding out against the bombs of the Luftwaffe, although at that time there were a lot of people in and around Europe who did not know who exactly were dropping what on whom, and who defined the enemy loosely as anyone who can bring himself to drop bombs on people he does not even know.

But one had to be careful. Heroism, unlike intelligence, expects to be respected. If any pimp came out Maltese there would be at least one exiled compatriot who would march up and down the aisle of the theatre with a placard that reminded people of the George Cross and the Luftwaffe. So I made the pimp Welsh, knowing that no member of that nation would ever have the hard worldliness or initiative to engage in so tricky a calling.

From the beginning of the enterprise hints of doom flew like hail. To share the top billing with the pimp I introduced a journalist called Jim and an intelligent and vocal harlot called Mollie. In the first draft I made no attempt to give any great significance to these two. Like the rest of the cast they would serve as hooks for a few choric romps. But this did not suit Richard. Any great musical, he said, had to have a big, throbbing love interest to provide the inspiration for deathless tunes. Every time we met the first thing he asked me was how Jim and Mollie were getting on and I had to be reminded of who they were.

This insistence on a love theme went right against the grain. From the moment I started to write I had proceeded according to certain rough commandments. Thou must not advocate war; in a time when dominant scientists seem to have little idea of what the hell they are up to, inaccuracy must be regarded as a possible source of salvation. Try always to reduce the lagoon of trash that surrounds the concept of romantic love. I was so

fanatical on the last point that I had written to the Society of
Authors to command its members to grant the libido a ten-year
rest. So it was with sorrow that I felt myself giving ground
before Richard's campaign to have the affair between Jim
and Mollie grow to red-hot intensity. I would not have felt
more embarrassed if I had stepped on them carnally active in a
park.

Every time Richard left one of our numberless conferences
he was smiling. He had dragged out of me a few more pages for
Jim and Mollie. They were to represent the tenderest act of pas-
sion since Tristan and Isolde or Broken Blossoms. I kept look-
ing for the hole in the floor through which sanity would appear
to have slipped. More than once I felt like pulling off a coup
exploiting the dockside background. It was to rewrite the play
with Jim and Mollie being found washed up in Number Five
berth, drowned and beyond singing. But Richard, in just one
more conference, would have introduced a number featuring the
kiss of life, and the two lovers would have been as limber as
ever.

If I raised a tiny fist of rejection in a bid to stem the stream
of goo, Richard would sit patiently, praise my splendid memory
and coax me into a rendering, in a slow, sad baritone of the
ripest love melodies of the century's great musicals, 'Love Holds
the Key to Set Me Free', 'One Alone to be My Own', 'Some
Enchanted Evening', 'Tonight, Tonight', 'Ah, Sweet Mystery of
Life', to remind me that if I could generate the right sort of
tingle in the wires uniting Jim and Mollie that would be the
fuel needed by the composer to produce the sort of swooning
items that would give the piece a longer run than *Chu Chin
Chow*.

I would mutter that if we had a grain of sense we would geld
Jim, launch Mollie on a Teachers' Training course and concen-
trate all our fire on building up the pimp and his flanking
platoon of gamblers, drinkers, fighters and hustlers. But I lost
every time. Love had found a way, right over the dead body of
my defeated will.

As soon as the book ground to what both Richard and I

thought should be a halt, the music started rolling off the belt. Richard was enthusiastic about the composer's genius. He had, he said, a turn for atonality, a talent for tragic discord which would have Schoenberg and Orff queueing up to take credit for 'You Are My Sunshine'. I met the composer and his wife for tea in a Cardiff hotel. He was gifted but unconfident. She had a rigid sense of dedication to his career that made Lady Macbeth look like a fumbler.

She asked me what kind of music I envisaged for the show. Oh, instantly tuneful, I said. A joyful rejigging of some Welsh folk-songs, hymns, especially the hymns of Sankey and Moody, the American evangelists, whose words and melodies are still loud in the minds of those old enough to have witnessed the whole final stage of crack-up in the religious life of our land. (It is a big part of the Welsh ethic to believe that with the lapse of the chapels a light of paradise drained out of Welsh life. Many of the people who hold this view would, if promised a return to their old dominion by the religious ministers, emigrate to Baffin Bay.)

Tunes, I told the composer's wife, that would bring a smile to the heavy lips of the Black and White Minstrels. She looked disgusted. She raised a dripping crumpet and I would not have been surprised if she had let me have one with it. She said that if I expected her husband to follow slavishly in the wake of Puccini or *Oklahoma*, I was in for total disappointment. He was his own spirit and he would utterly ignore the banality of my own conceptions as revealed in the book.

The choreography was hectic and struck the same note of desperate striving as the rest of the work. Rehearsals were held in a central London Y.M.C.A. and the cast would not have been put through a more bitter set of physical paces if they had been intended to storm the Menai Straits and seize Anglesey. Fencing, swimming, wrestling, climbing, not a single ploy was spared to bring the players up to a peak of commando fitness. Rehearsals started early. The actors were an amiably beer-loving group and more than half of them were convinced that the musical existed only as a cover beneath which they would be broken by exertion, and forced out of an overcrowded profession by break-down and madness.

There were whole patches of the action that brought back memories of the Somme. The actors, musing over their glasses of light ale, showed the blinks and twitches of incipient shell-shock. When they walked they now tended to jump and cavort, and the fencing had their arms moving in a way that spilled a lot of beer. One of them told me the effects of swordsman-ship, diving and duels with Japanese staves on his domestic life had driven his wife into the attic.

There was a sequence that called for the leading actress, a soprano, to be dandled on the handles of six brushes. One of the actors, shorter than the others, could get no smoothness in-to this movement, and he kept jabbing at the soprano to ensure for his broom a firmer grip, a tactic that caused a lot of distress and talk.

Bodily I would say they were all in before the curtain was due to go up. The week before the show was due to open Richard gave the male members of the cast a nice meal in Wardour Street. The dessert provided the evening's only hint of sweet-ness. The men were solidly behind the viewpoint of their spokesman. They criticised the book, the music, the dancing. Had there been a separate corps de ballet their spines might be showing fewer splits, but our group had to do the sing-ing, the dancing and the delivery of some pretty complex dialogue.

I said nothing. They knew my mood. I was waiting for the answer to an advertisement I had put in a paper asking what had happened to Sankey and Moody and the Black and White Minstrels. And I had heard with my own ears the result on them of swinging into a vigorous chorus within a second or two of ending a severe jig. The first sound that came from them was like a death-rattle, dramatically arresting, but not relevant to the theme which dealt with the rosier delights of living.

The spokesman said that they would withdraw their labour if the production was not humanised to suit the gifts of fairly mature Celts who, physically, had lost their primal sharpness. Richard sat attentive, smiling, nodding, totally sympathetic.

On the following Monday the show opened in Blackpool. Everything was totally unchanged, except that the brush-routine had been modified to allow the soprano to come through the season with at least one spinal disc unslipped. The show's name was *Loud Organs*. The phrase came from the hymnal: 'Loud organs, their story forth tell in deep tones.' I had been told that picking the title of a play from a hymn would bring every bit as much bad luck as spilling salt or passing through a bishop's legs without touching his gaiters. I agreed. You cannot define the sources of bad luck without being consistently right.

The audience at the opening night consisted mainly of guest-house landladies taking their first rest at the end of a packed summer. Ticket prices might also have been cut for them, for it is hard to lure these ladies into a theatre except with a burlesque show of broad appeal, chorines and jests with obvious ends. The title *Loud Organs* might have attracted them. Spoken in a certain tone and a bit of fiddling with the eyebrows, it can conjure up the idea of a simple-witted salacity of the type that startles the ozone in pier-end shows.

They were foxed. Between whiffs of subversion in the dialogue and blasts of modernism in the score, they were ready after the first five minutes to go out with the next tide. After the first act most of them drifted out to buy a poisoned prawn sandwich and to take their place in the queue for the following day's organ recital and community singing at the Tower Ballroom, a cultural trump in the hand of this strange resort.

It was a bad week for the already harassed cast. Blackpool was the worst possible place for them. It is a town of devices meant to cozen, humiliate but eventually to recharge a moron. For the rest it breeds a despair about the human situation that only suicide or artificial hormones can relieve. By mid-week their spirits could be heard crunching among the trodden cockles of the seaside sidewalks.

One of the cast claimed that he had seen Tommy Steele at one of the matinées rolling in the aisle. I discounted this. At certain hours of the day a lot of people can look like Tommy Steele, and motives for rolling in aisles and elsewhere can be various. Also, the member of the cast, a laggard singer and an inept dancer, who claimed to have spotted Steele, was at the end of his tether and was in a state where, with a little prompting, he might have seen anyone, and clearly.

When the company left Blackpool on the Sabbath, their next stop was Cardiff, and the word stop in the context had terrifying overtones. Cardiff, theatrically, is as dispiriting as Bass Rock, a place long on gales and gannets and deprived to cemetery point of living people. But after Blackpool it had the sound, the smell, the prospect of Canaan. The show ran there for a fortnight. I saw it in full for the first time. Like the Blackpool landladies I was left puzzled. It joined the mountain in the middle of my life made up of things that have made no sense. Groups of Nationalists, temporarily deprived of detonators to blow things up, booed the piece with fervour, and the booing, together with the acoustics of the New Theatre, traditionally fitful, ensured for the rest of the audience an almost complete lack of communication. As I was leaving the theatre, a woman, speaking to no one in particular, said, 'Well, did that leave you any the wiser?' I was the first to reply. 'No,' I said and bought her a compensatory drink.

It moved for a last week to Brighton. Short of setting up road-blocks and gun emplacements, the refusal to allow it entry into London's West End could not have been more firmly stated. The Brighton audiences became hostile only to take the chill off their indifference. Even the fish, getting as close to the expensive sea front as they can afford, complained that the humans were carrying their indifference too far. The alienation effect was so complete the ushers remained seated or disguised. Some of the more sensitive fossils of this traditionalist stronghold still believe that the show was a sinister portent of the epoch of socialist misrule that was shortly to befall them.

The organs, never very loud, fell silent. The leading soprano, sick and tired of being dandled on six broom-ends by six of the jerkiest joggers ever to occupy a stage, bought the brooms and

burned them to make quite sure she would never again be in-
volved in such an antic. The actors took their place at the shell-
shock entrance of the nearest Theatrical Exchange. Myself, a
lust for silence welling up from every part of me, looked up
Trappists in the directory.

5
See one miracle and you've seen the lot

Hanging around as a subordinate crumb on television has the discontinuity and tedium of trying to carry on a conversation with a slow horse. One stumbles around, quite agreeing with the cold eyes of TV stage technicians telling you to drop flat and dead. One subserves a web of electronic wires, great enough to hang all humanity, and one day it might do just that.

TV is insatiably nosy. To feed its demand for novelty it burrows indecently. Just as one feels when surveying our platoon of sweating comics that there just is not enough laughter to go around, no one feels in the face of television that there is simply not enough life to go around, yours or anyone else's.

If you want to qualify for a lifebelt of benzedrine, then try a little TV commentary and interviewing. The hazards are immense. One of my first efforts was in a magazine programme, shot live, of Britain's mighty industrial heart. One of the valves was a South Wales steel works. I was to provide a verbal backdrop for a four- or five-minute glimpse of a furnace being tapped. I was planted on some hellishly exposed contraption directly above the smelters.

I had the cinematic tradition of Fritz Lang on my right hand and a forty-foot drop on my left. I got the sign for action and started on my talk. 'Move up, Mount Etna,' or some such flat-footed fatuity. After a few seconds I was motioned to dry up. London had decided to cut us out altogether and switch to another line of country; we were dropped dead. There are still some people in South Wales who saw and heard that pointless interlude and who are still not convinced that it had anything to do with a terrestrially produced TV programme. They think that the sight of flame and the simultaneous sound of my voice are some new form of neurotic Calvinistic tic. There are times when I think so myself.

Then there was that day of autumn monsoon in Porthcawl, a seaside fun centre in South Wales. I was to put in some of the words at the televising of a carnival jazz-band competition. As the soaked and wind-whipped bands marched into the arena I plunged into one of the jerkiest spiels in the history of commentary. I had to interview the five-year-old mascot of some band dressed as British Grenadiers. This child had been marching in front of the band and looked pretty glassy by the time he reached me. Between being drenched, a surfeit of candy floss, being concussed by the heavy tread of the Grenadiers behind him, then having me looming over him with a face that had lost the last of its friendly charm hours before, his mind was well muffled. Our dialogue was straight out of 'Dragnet'.

'What's your name?'

'Basil.'

'How long have you been dressed up in this way?'

'Basil.'

'Why Grenadiers? What's the motivation here? How does this square with the basic anti-militarism of the Welsh?'

'Basil.'

And so on.

I got a medallion as the interviewer least likely ever to put a foot wrong, being unable to get the foot started in the first place.

Then I made some remarks about a mixed band of Matadors from Maesteg. The boys came first. Wanting to flash off my knowledge of the corridas, I said, 'I'd like to see a full-grown Miura bull loose among that lot.' I should have been looking at the monitor screen. The camera was on the girls.

Then came a band of women dressed as harem-girls, nautch-girls or some type of Eastern concubine. It was the most daring hint of the boudoir in the public life of the Celts. The wind blew their flimsy satin robes into high relief. There was only one man in this band. He was a drummer, forlorn and so depleted he could hardly get his sticks to the pigskin. The cameras went switching on to all the wrong women, and there was I trying to provide a verbal pattern that would fit into a moral context.

You will find a passionate urge in the most peculiar people to squeeze on to the small screen. We are familiar with the incredible performers who turn up as competitors in the more rudimentary quiz-shows: i.e. 'Give me the name of a statesman whose name contains the word "church".' The poor morlock, who probably needs a guide dog to get him beyond the sports page, thinks, blinks, winks to lift the tension and says: 'All-church.'

But tragedy can be subtler than that. On one programme we were to find a railway station somewhere in the North Glamorgan hills on the night of a rugby international being played between Wales and England in London. The station had to be empty because the whole point was to show the English viewers that almost the entire population of the town had gone madly wantoning off to the big game.

Plans were made to lock up those citizens who might want to come on to the platform and spoil the forlorn effect. A train was to pull into the station. I was to step off and a porter would shuffle out of the gloom which is very good along that part of the track. The porter carries a lantern and hums an old Welsh hymn to show that he is sad at not being in or around

Sussex Gardens, Paddington, drinking, singing and whooping with the boys. I ask him why the place is so deserted. He tells me.

He had rehearsed. Before the broadcast he went around the valleys warning all his relations to watch the screen on the big night. The day before the show, a gale blew down the radio link that was to help the limping item over the hills. The station interview was out. The production team drew lots to decide who should tell the porter. He himself by this time was also drawing lots to decide whether he would wear his hair like Gilbert Harding or Perry Como. It took a long time to make him realise that the news of the cancellation was not just a dodge to bring his talent up to concert pitch. Then he shuffled back into the shadows and it took the hope-and-resignation talk of six Sunday School superintendents to prevent him from sending away for the hara-kiri pamphlet in the Do-It-Yourself series.

My most thorough exposure to the cameras came when I sat in as one of the sages on the B.B.C. Brains Trust. Its personnel is made up in the main of aristocrats, polymaths, tycoons and arch-administrators. No one has more emphatically been none of these things than I. In family terms my father was a social incompetent. In terms of learning I have run unsteadily around the outposts of European culture and could barely have a stab at defining the fences that divide Bevan from Buddha. As a tycoon, I could look back on three weeks' work in Selfridges in some type of toy-stall. In the first two weeks I drove Claus bald and almost brought the Christmas trade to a halt.

True, I had written some novels, but I was strictly a non-Establishment hillman looking in while ostensibly looking out. I would search through my brain like oakum for some fact that would jolt the complacency of the polymaths. As an almanack, my pages hadn't even been cut. I had never watched a bird, cross-bed a fruit-fly, nor picked over an ancient site; my refusal to believe that algebra was really there had sent three teachers hurtling into the Taff, my home river. I had never caused an explosion. I was way behind. In India I would not even have been allowed to cast my shadow on anybody. In that company you-need to be as cool as an arctic seal not to feel like sending home for your leper's bell and hood.

That smooth flow of eloquence, assurance and charm was too rich for the blood. Each Monday evening after a Sunday session I would sit over an antidotal pint with three of the most consummate and neurasthenic clucks in the vale of Morgannwg just to get back a whiff of bemusement.

The reactions of most people to my fitful appearances were interesting. From some, a dumb wonderment that a local boy was up there on Sinai. 'I bet you've got to read all the way up on the train, to be ready for them.' Others would assume that I had now become a kind of public lantern, prescient, compassionate, omnicompetent, like the accepted public image of God; they would demand from me the winner of the Derby or the whereabouts of a pigeon or a wife that had failed to return to the loft. I would tell them.

I uncovered also some exceptional seams of malice especially among drunks whose resentments were beginning to mortify and threaten. This programme, it would appear, sets off the most enormous yearning among the more bumptious of our morons. These people would sullenly question my qualifications to be up there in Delphi. A Cecil they could take, but not an untitled Thomas. A magnate they could see the point of, but not a very ordinary sort of schnook who went into banks only to get out of the rain.

Once in a while I would have a spasm of self-defensive shame with these people. I would hint that in spite of my proletarian overtones we had somewhere in our family the natural son of Nesta, that nymphomanic princess of Pembrokeshire. We had kept this dark because as a family we disliked talking about sex. Also, I made clear the apparent poverty of my boyhood had been a pose, a mask of destitution put on in order to make the surrounding paupers feel at ease. As for wealth, I would have them know, as I had told my landlady in my freezing phase at Oxford, that my father had not left the coal trade as a redundant miner; he had simply pulled his money out of the bituminous market when the Navy went over to oil and the poor

M

went over to coolness. Two people believed me, but they had just had a session on plonk, a brew of port, lanoline, ale and gorsedd juice.

Punditry in any shape or place is a base act. The ability to pontificate in public on a wide range of unlike subjects should involve a man in a kind of breathalyser test in reverse. If he has done it without being loaded above a certain alcoholic level he should be put down on grounds of brazen arrogance.

That I should ever have got mixed up in it was quite against the run of my nature. I suffer from an ingrained duplicity of mind which consistently causes me to change my viewpoint in the middle of a sentence. My brain is a kind of spinning Janus. I would have made a good second-line man for any politician suffering from too many over-exposed insincerities. Halfway through the enumeration of any dogma I leap to embrace its exact opposite. I shrink away from certainty with the instinct that draws any sensible animal away from excessive heat. I am a walking antidote to any sort of papal complacency. At my birth infallibility should have been heard giving out its last apologetic gasp. I have a belief in the abounding fertility of folly or foolishness, not to make too big a thing of it, and that is about all.

Also, the onset of what most of us call wisdom is little more than a rusting over of parts of the brain made wet by tears of angry protest shed soon and violently. Up to a certain age there exists a passionate response to grief, a moral copulation of immense force. Every wound visible on the flesh of the species comes in for its hourly sympathetic rub, until the agent of pity becomes nearly as much of a nuisance as the initial maker of the wounds.

After thirty we are cooling fools. Too much blood has gone out with the compassion and we hear rumours that anaemia kills. Beliefs that had attained a tentative firmness liquesce and are lost. We rush through a hastening dusk, lusting for midnight.

Nothing changes. The pot-bellied tolerance of Buddhism blocks the road to every raging enthusiasm and prejudice that

scalded the heart of yesterday. Nothing matters: nothing
changes. Crime and idiocy remain constant in every generation.
Guilt and innocence are interchangeable masks, idiot eyes in a
dying head. Opposites are little more than malign reflections.
We are victims, one and all, of a mirror's malicious magic, fair-
ground starers whose hopes, along with hair, move towards
their climactic dandruff. We have become weightless and
not even convinced that we are speeding towards the right
moon.

Punishment is presumptuous nonsense, judges our most
sinister and superfluous adornment. The liver-fluke has as much
right to the sheep as we have. Taste and fastidiousness are
tedious traps: envy the fly that alights with equal joy on dia-
mond or dung. Solicitude is a sclerotic nuisance. Get hot under
the collar and some other innocent neck will burn. Stop your
flushes of concern about the colour-bar. When our present stock
of superficial lunacies have been scraped away, be sure that a
new set of nightmares waits to move in. Convert our deserts
into high-walled clinics for our colour-conscious clowns, ghastly
official distinctions about the mental fitness of each and every
one of us will come along to make our present neuroses about
racial differences seem like nothing at all. D. H. Lawrence is
alive in Abersychan, self-castrated, praising income-tax, at ease
at last and a grinning darts-player and bingo-addict. And God
Save the Pound, love, Gypsy Moth the Fourth, hallucinogenic
fungi, and Mitch Fitch and his Itching Bitches.

Now this is a poor mood for anyone ambitious to become a
catherine-wheel in any sort of Brains Trust. Indifference, flip-
pancy, mercurial changes of view as the imagination flips the
facts into new and daft perspectives, all these are fatal. The
thing to do is to run on the hot feet of concern from one talk-
ing point to the next: flower-power, flogging, liberated
pederasts, elderly aldermen, immigration, promiscuity, pollu-
tion, the whole boiling stew-pot of our perplexities and pouts.
Or a slow, judicial earnestness that comes within whispering
distance of idiocy. Verbal controversy is the authentic human
trademark and it should be given its due. If you are paid for it

one should make some small polite gesture at the cash that comes one's way.

Time and again I would try to align my performance with one or other of these ideals: the bright-eyed omniscience of the scoutmaster, or the leaden authority of the Supreme Court judge. But I could never match the smooth integrity of my colleagues. Other people's gravity goes to my head faster than brandy. The chairman's first words always seemed to shake my screws loose. Every phrase I uttered invoked in my own mind a shower of blinding reservations. The *volte-faces* came along so fast a large part of the audience turned to face the back wall with a view to anticipating my next manœuvre.

I would hear the chairman say, 'Now a subject I'm sure we've touched on before. Blood sports. Especially fox-hunting.' The chairman is right. Fox-hunting is so inevitable a topic in English panel discussions the last pre-programme drink is a stirrup cup and the last mutual good wishes a horned halloo. On hearing the chairman's remark my interest would not be stirred. My life has been so utterly horseless, so totally foxless, I would be convinced that no one would have the nerve to put the question to me first.

But nerve is what chairmen are bound to have if they are going to milk a little sapience out of four assorted and anxious strangers. The chairman's eye would light on me as if led on to the target by borrowed hounds. 'Thomas, what do you feel about this?' In the first moment of helplessness native to a man who has long since hauled down the flags of political and philosophic assurance, I would be tempted to say that my father, in the forty-ninth slump of his life, had lost his last horse and eaten his last fox. Then I would have a mental image of the spurred and hooting fellows of our sporting countryside, who scare hell out of their two-legged and four-legged inferiors, and my first verdict came out in a sullen bass mumble. 'Hunters should be hunted.'

Then the wig would twitch and in went the switch. 'Oh, no. That's wrong. I shouldn't have said that. Stupid prejudice. Inverted snobbery, as the editorials say. Let them hunt. Leave them to it. If they weren't after foxes, God knows what they'd be up to. To each and every one of us, Sade writes his own peculiar postcard.'

I suppose the model for anyone wishing to make it on the symposium front is Dr Jacob Bronowski. He is one of the marvels of the contemporary mind, a distinguished polymath and a rich legend. Without strain he could give you the weight of the moon and the proportion of turpentine poured by your father into his second tin of paint for his second try at interior decoration.

He is almost total intelligence. One's eyes tend to concentrate on his head, convinced that the rest of him will not dare to match the splendour of that temple. He came to Britain from Poland at the age of nine, a refugee from pogroms and speaking only Polish. He read his way through the large library of the bright and literate London slum where he settled. In the shortest possible time he was at Cambridge confounding the older sages with his cool and sure insights. He is the classic product of twentieth-century Europe and it was logical that, at a certain point of ripeness, he should move to America, to Dr Salk's omnivalent clinic on the West Coast, where a lot of life's more acute mysteries are being made blunter and more amenable. The best minds, like the most ruthless bodies, have a westward bent.

He was an almost indispensable pillar of the B.B.C. Television Brains Trust, its most sybilline mouth. For a comparable figure you would have to go back to Dr Cyril Joad, the sound radio version of the same programme. All the sessions of those distant panels can still be heard on about two dozen long-playing records. I listened to them all and I would recommend them to anyone interested in the convolutions of punditry, its greatnesses, its black gulfs and astonishing follies. One emerges from the experience with permanently cross-eyed thoughts, and at least one eroded ear.

Dr Joad was the philosopher who took a birch to the woollier aspects of semantics and demanded, in every question, an inquiry into the words involved and their basic meaning, hostile to any suggestion that the wool of ambivalency on most of our utterances is a protective covering, essential to life and not a dirty device to be stripped off and discarded.

Joad's was the most penetrating voice ever raised in Britain, the centre of the wool trade in every respect, demanding an aseptic sanity. Towards the end of his life he was tripped up and shamed by a couple of run-of-the-mill ironies. He appeared in court charged with trying to defraud a railway company by travelling on a used ticket, and he died of nothing less fundamental than a rectal cancer.

I don't suppose the mythic element of Dr Bronowski's own life would make any appeal to him at all. In his book one plays a game of high ideas, using the most lucid media, while trying not to be disturbed by the forgivable and largely curable aberrants who prowl around the earth.

Sloppiness in any shape or form he deplores. I told him the story of a villageful of restless peasants in northern Italy who wanted to get to America at a time when these migrations were easy and cheap. The local landlord was excessively sour and the local grapes had followed suit. They wished a blight on the landlord and got ready to go. They knew as little of geography as of social justice, but they had heard that Chicago was a growing place and full of Italians and flesh-markets. They fell into the hands of a phony travel agent. He told them he would see them safe in Illinois and took from them the full fare.

They began the journey. They were surprised at the narrowness of the Atlantic and the brevity of their journey from New York to the Middle West. New York turned out to be Cardiff and they found themselves in a place called Treorchy, a small but busy township at the head of the Rhondda Valley. Some of them, still convinced that no compatriot of theirs could be such a scamp as that travel agent, are still there saluting Lincoln and looking for the stockyards.

Dr Bronowski, as he pondered the probabilities of this tale, was not amused. There is little room in his universe for suckers. If he made the journey from Cracow to London at the age of nine, those silly Lombardians could have been expected to show some comparable ability. America, he said, saddled by a fine crop of troubles already, was lucky not to have been visited by such a batch of morons. I do not think that he could ever have instantly perceived that this was a story made up simply to pass a little time.

Fiction is odious to him and writers of fiction a suspect lot. Tales meant to entertain are for him uncollected refuse along a potentially handsome and admirable street. I can still recall his look of chilly astonishment when I suggested that a story like *Treasure Island* was comparable in neatness and as capable of giving delight as any of those laboratory demonstrations in physics where men rub rods and give them strange life, sparking, magnetising, and so on. For him I think I was always somewhat outside the pale. He once mentioned, and his tone was grudging, that a lady in Cheltenham, who had read some of my novels, wished to send me her good wishes. 'Of course, I never read novels.' His expression implied that he would never have the same opinion of the Cheltenham lady again.

At that moment I was suffering from writer's cramp, writer's block and minstrel's crouch. I told him that, in the matter of novels, it was a pity we could not all be that lucky. I felt a sense of shock, feeling his remark to be a betrayal of my belief in The Lie as a Compulsory Social Tactic. If I had ever been introduced to Jack the Ripper I would, for the sake of charm and amity, have congratulated him on certain side benefits of his main activity, such as profits to cutlers and crime writers. The attempt politely to deflate the significance of another person's activity I take to be a most unfragrant gambit.

I was reminded of an occasion when I took part in one of those summer schools meant to enlarge the intellectual banks of the industrial proletariat. One of the students was a militant railwayman, his face blazing with rancour, his shoulders a barricade of chips. He regarded me as having, in some elfin way, slapped the revolution across the face and caused some of the weaker toilers to view their own best dreams with doubt. As he shook my hand, his shoulder stiffened and the chips formed fours and gave a hostile salute.

'I'm warning you now,' he said. 'I'm a convinced Marxist and a railwayman. I'm in charge of the Birchtown signal box. An essential hub of any transport system, the signal box. No time for trifles. Between the cunning of the masters and the apathy of the slaves, I've got to see that the right ideas keep moving. Like a signal box, see? So, I'm giving you warning now, before the lecturing starts. I haven't read any of your bloody books.'

'That's all right,' I said. 'I haven't seen any of your bloody signals either.'

I don't think Dr Bronowski ever accorded me any clear identity. Had he been more aware of me I feel his attitude towards me would have been even more dismissive. But his consciousness of other people was so short in range, he looked at most people as if he had just rejected them from a theorem, and he looked at me as if I had never got into it. Sensing me to be unscientific, dedicated to viewing life as a spinning and mostly hilarious disorder, he saw little point in me and would have taken a more respectful interest in my being had I been a badger ambling and blinking from its hole and asking the television boys to switch to whores because the lights bother it.

After he had met me several times he had no clear idea of who I was. Twice we shook hands in the private reception room at Scott's in Piccadilly, the peerless oyster place, and he said, 'Ah, Dr Glyn Daniel. Delighted to meet you.' Dr Daniel is an eminent Cambridge archaeologist, a native of Wales, whose face is as nationally well known as any in Britain. His eyes and eyebrows and mine have a vaguely similar Celtic cut but, apart from that, we are as clearly distinguishable as Vernon Brody and the Venerable Bede. (Brody was a wrestler and not venerable.)

When the Doctor made this mistake of identity for the second time, I still stood in such awe of his infallibility my will caved in and I told myself he must be right and that I must be Glyn Daniel. In any case, in that strange ambience I felt like a change of image. I prepared a short statement on my latest dig in the burial chambers of north Britanny, one of Dr Daniel's favourite areas of research. Then my mind went into its usual perverse double shuffle and I said firmly that I was not Dr Glyn Daniel and had never probed the burial secrets of the Ancient Celt. No. I was Harry Secombe, the well-known Welsh comedian and tenor. The sage turned away from me without a word and I heard him tell one of the other panellists that he thought it a destructive error on the part of the producer to invite people like professional funsters on to a programme that was supposed intellectually to have a serious aim.

He had it in for comedians. Not long afterwards he threatened to withdraw from the programme if Bernard Braden, the clever Canadian satirist, was to be nominated chairman of the Trust. I have the feeling that the final triumph of science and technology will be to have humour classified as a kind of racial stigma and stage a genocide of jokers. In so many respects laughter and love are the arts of the inept and the inaccurate, the sloppy lot who will be edged out of the picture when we are all finally corralled in the pitiless plans of the bureaucrats and bombardiers, who will join in fiendish wedlock the dreams of maximum productivity and the fact of maximum waste.

The small core of humanism in the heart of contemporary science, left over from the old-fashioned omnilateral ideal of education, is an asset that will shrink more and more swiftly in the face of our most appalling alliance of the scientist and the soldier, both creatures so socially imperfect they can behold prospects of desolation without blinking an eye.

But the Doctor's skill as a dialectician will always stay high on my list of admirations. Watching his eyes you could see behind them the processes of analysis, selection and exposition operating like the tumblers of a great safe. The miracle was almost audible. It might have had something to do with the plateful of oysters he ate with thoughtful relish at the pre-programme lunch, but this suspicion is not worth a moment of one's time. I tried a plateful of oysters myself to see if I could hoist myself up a magisterial inch or two. All that happened was that my stomach felt as if it were wearing a rubber suit and my mind packed up for an hour or two. Most of the questions that afternoon seemed to be about the Arctic, one of my poorest subjects, and between ignorance and oysters I looked and sounded a loon.

During the programme he could behave with a calm detachment that had one leaning forward from time to time to make sure he was still there. The average harum-scarum panellist played the game according to simple rules. The circulating ball would land at his feet and he would kick it. He was rarely overwhelmed by the feeling that he was chiselling a mint-fresh tablet up there on Sinai.

Not so the Doctor. His posture of elevation was so extreme you would not have been surprised if his nose bled. He often nodded his head in serene withdrawal when his turn came around to further the joust. He reminded me of a very self-centred sage back in my valley of whom it was said that he only ceased to be an agnostic when he found that he himself was God.

The Doctor would wait until the rest of us had, in full mental disarray, yammered out our footling opinions. He would smile and watch us dripping with disgrace. Then he would lay a gigantic wreath of logic on our shallow graves, enumerating our fallacies and his own truths. His thoughts glittered like Cartier's window. He held his hands in front of him, the finger-tips touching as if guarding a shrine of golden perceptions.

At those lunches at Scott's the talk could be heady for someone who had got no nearer the corridors of power than the outside toilet where in-fighting, even of the cleverest kind, goes for nothing. Many potent people from the worlds of business, education, Civil Service, took their places there. At that table the theme of preferment was as common as bread on the tables of the poor. The names of the brilliant arrivistes in the under-thirties group were sieved, arranged and presented for the inspection of those who had patronage to bestow. One saw the face of Britain's meritocracy for the next two decades forming before one's eyes and one felt little optimism. A million individual attitudes, all righteously convinced of their sapience, were glued together to create the unique tradition of ungifted management that has kept peacetime Britain at half-cock since the end of the first world war. And it will take the glue a long time to give up.

Take a glittering working-class son of a left-wing militant parent, and after twenty years of lush fulfilment he will be emulating and admiring all the people his father loathed. It is, I suppose, a kind of nitrogen cycle, a wise recognition of the toxic quality of passionate phobias and the need, once in a lucky while, to make them seem absurd and cut them short.

It was a relief to get back from the arch-revelations of intrigue and ineptitude of high places and talk without any special sense of responsibility about the dead, who could not be disquieted or hurt and would not, in normal conditions, turn up on television. There was one occasion which yielded a fair patch of conversational oddity. The Doctor and I were sitting together and talking about his own excellent book on William Blake, the mystic poet and subversive etcher.

On my right hand was Lady Violet Bonham Carter, daughter of Earl Asquith, leader of British Liberalism in its golden age before David Lloyd George planted a boot in the class-relationships of the old party by grafting on to it the conscience of a village radical. Try joining Holland House to a Welsh chapel vestry, the gambling, guzzling spirit of Charles James Fox to that of a Welsh Sabbatarian and something is bound to crack. Lloyd George, in ways so devious he might yet appear in history books as three other people, tried it and he cracked. The sound of it still dements the more naive of his worshippers in all parts of Britain.

Lady Violet does not like Lloyd George even in recollection. She regarded him as a garrulous, ill-bred chap, pathologically envious and sly. Some part of this judgment rubs off on any Welshman she speaks to. More than once she left me fingering the dents in my ego and vowing to forswear adjectives, lilting perorations and snap judgments.

She has become over the years, largely through television, a keystone of cool graciousness and a reproach to the flushed and

182 A few selected exits

shoddy world in which she lives. On that afternoon she was
sitting next to Alan Bullock, Master of St Catherine's College,
Oxford, and biographer of those two rough dogmatists and
sextons of Bolshevism, Hitler and Ernest Bevin, both par-
tially educated men of immense energy who proved that
ignorance can be fun. Philosophically Alan Bullock is one of
our most interesting archivists. He emerged from a world of
Conservative preferences to take a deep, creative interest in men
who have served on various levels as agents of change.

Lady Violet and he were discussing a book that had appeared
the previous week. The author of this book was Robert Blake,
one of the remarkable group of younger historians to have
emerged recently to feed a vast contemporary appetite about
the period 1880–1920, the seed-bed of most current mischief.
The subject of the book was Bonar Law, a strange, withdrawn
man who was dragged from the process of a quiet dying to spear-
head the Conservative assault that sent Lloyd George toppling
after Asquith into oblivion. Oblivion in Britain, as in America,
is clogged with Liberals who never quite knew how they
perished.

Lady Violet mentioned an anecdote related in the book which
had Bonar Law motoring down from London with Lord
Beaverbrook to put some bit of inspired pressure on Asquith.
Beaverbrook was one of the sharper draughts in British politics,
a whistling Svengali, who all his life through was astonished to
find so many of his dummies excessively alive and vocal. They
waited a long time to see Asquith. He was not available, and
away they went, empty-handed. Robert Blake claimed that As-
quith had been doing nothing more significant than playing
cards, and a fairly trivial game at that. It typified the brazen
indolence that most of our elderly statesmen have worn like a
shell, soft, urbane but utterly life-defying.

The story had annoyed Lady Violet. She denounced it as a
slur on her father. She remembered the incident well. That
morning her father had been presented with two punnets of
plums. They were a type of plum to which he was addicted. He
ate the lot. They gave his bowels a sensational release. While

Bonar Law and Beaverbrook were waiting, he was utterly un-available. Had he presented himself to Bonar Law and Beaver-brook he would have been guilty of a frankness unacceptable to politicians. Playing cards had nothing to do with the case.

While Lady Violet was putting this bit of history right, the Doctor and I continued to discuss his book on William Blake. I congratulated him on being so masterly an analyst of the untidier forces in human experience like poetry and mysticism. I spoke of the incident of a visitor calling on Blake and his wife and finding them in a summer house reading *Paradise Lost* aloud to each other. They were both stark naked to under-line the primal innocence which is the subject of the poem. They sat there with nothing between them and the visitor but Mil-ton's text and in such an ecstasy of communication it took some tapping on the glass panes of the conservatory to get them out of Eden.

Lady Violet paused and listened. She heard me mention Blake. In a mood of exposition she is remarkably single-minded and she assumed that the Blake I was talking about was the Robert Blake who had written the book about Bonar Law. (This story is of the sort that needs a policeman to supplement the traffic-lights.) 'Blake?' she said, with that marvellous move-ment of the nose and mouth that suggests a damning analyst's report on the whole post-Asquithian world. 'What about him?' 'Naked,' I said. 'In an arbour. Reading *Paradise Lost*. To his wife. She was naked too, and reading.'

She nibbled a bit of cheese like a taster getting ready for a new flavour.

'It's credible,' she said. 'A man starts spreading inaccuracies about my father and ends up reading Milton in an arbour, un-clothed.'

Only once did the Doctor drop his veil and reveal some of the perplexity that might still prowl behind the assurance of the polymath. We were in a taxi to Paddington from the studios at Lime Grove where in pre-television days Lord Rank, the film and show-business tycoon, combined a wholesome piety with the making of formidably bad films.

The Doctor had been brooding over some acerb remarks directed at him and myself by Lady Violet for taking the side of the strikers in some recent dispute. The Doctor and I had suggested that the ostracising of strike-breakers was no more loathsome than the censure of deserters in the war. Lady Violet had come as near as her supreme urbanity would allow to calling us a pair of loons. The incident had led him to view me with a fleeting fellow-feeling. 'I suppose your background has had its share of unrest and menace,' he said, and went on to talk of the way his race had seemed to pass through corridors of miraculously suspended deaths, ghastly and almost unwanted survival.

I mumbled that compared with his people, mine, counting out the word-madness of our preachers, had had a picnic of it. He agreed and fell silent.

He moved his hands to take in the whole of London. 'A strange society,' he said. 'A bad society. I think that my race has persisted through an almost insane taste for abstinence, a fundamental dislike of life which, in some way, robbed life of some of its most destructive weapons. These people here will not be so lucky. Last Monday I called on some friends, a married couple. He was drunk. On Tuesday I called on them again. She was drunk. Now I'm sure you are like me about this. That kind of folly would have been absent from your tradition.'

My father had his last delirium registered in 1925. He was driven into restraint and virtue by credit running short and the coal trade running fast to the devil. But a taxi is no place to be saying things like that. And at that moment I felt an imperative need to be agreeing with one of the best brains we have.

The last time we met I offended him by the expression of some intemperate opinions to which I had given very little thought. I had said that in a lot of mathematical and scientific thinking I seemed to see veins of a quite oppressive banality, a stunning lust for repetition that plays into the hands of machines and infant prodigies. I had heard triangles ache from lack of privacy. Anyone, I finished in a burst of rancorous confidence, who discouraged the literary imagination—sole giver of lubricant self-suspicion—should be registered as a grave-digger.

The Doctor circled around me for an effortless kill. He told me that the culture I was prepared to go along with and regard as adequate had been starved of certain sensual revelations. Given three weeks, he said, he would teach even a mind like mine to respond to the rhythms of the great mathematical processes.

The prospect kept me depressed for a month. But it never came off. Mathematically, I am still a virgin and not a single ravisher in sight.

*

Someone had the idea that a television film about the Riviera would be in order. The sight of a screenful of sun-warmed flesh would be just the thing to relieve the bleakness of our watchers' lives on a wintry night. It was not a new idea: it is about as old as flesh, but television has given it a formidable extra spread, more so than the cinema, where there are ushers and other patrons to prevent people from suddenly crowding around the screen for a closer look. The sight of bosoms, bare and pendulous, bouncing along to this climax or that in African tribal revels has converted whole nations to anthropology and shattered many icy acres of diaconal reserve. Besides, we were in the course of a hesitant and pouting spring and any line of escape looked good.

We went to Cannes. The Film Festival was on and we assumed there would be plenty of beauty willing to exhibit. There was. As the swallows are reputed to rally at Capistrano, so had the starlets answered the call at Cannes. Shapeliness and ambition packed every boulevard and pier in the place. Ageing film producers covered their baldness with wigs, their faded eyeballs with luminous paint and searched among the throng for the first of the elect to be awarded the accolade of a mattress and a contract.

Thousands of tanned girls, in tediously full view just inside puberty, posed motionless on the beach flanked by mothers, predators by proxy, waiting for the influential glance that would hoist their young ones into the Sophia Loren set. Herds of cameramen blew on their eroded trigger fingers, ordering their models into variations on lasciviousness that would eventually have bored even the sensitive Adam. Morals and spinal discs could be heard slipping south in long, rattling cadences. Against the background of Cannes one could be excused for thinking that mothers, setting their infants strutting for sale, and photographers are two of the more serious flaws in our society.

I could barely see the Mediterranean for the aspects of vanity and corruption that filled the shore. My middle-aged hangover had a gala day. In moments of fatigue I would sink into a café chair and have a moralistic convulsion washed down with a bottle of Perrier. I joined hands over the centuries with John Knox and Lord Reith, those Elijhoid proponents of a laundered caution as life's best bet. (It is interesting that Lord Reith, our own contemporary version of God's appointed thunderer, should have so relented in the face of the world's temptation as to accept the flim-flam of a title, a mutilating obscenity if ever there was one. The only thing I cannot forgive Lady Chatterley for is her title. Perhaps it was thrown in to save the gamekeeper a bit of embarrassment. An association with the nobility is as robust an absurdity as those floral routines with which the lady and her lover tried to give an extra-pollinated edge and a certain element of surprise to sex.)

We were lucky in our hotel in Cannes. At about 11 p.m. it became as quiet as a funeral parlour of the less brash kind. It might have been that we were slow to look at or check on the time during the period of the festival when a bulging irrationality pushed out such anchoring concepts as noon and midnight. But we were glad of the calm that hit our hotel in late evening. We sat around waiting for drinks, but if the waiter charged with dispensing night-caps had been walking down from Paris and carrying the ingredients, they would not have taken longer to come.

The silence and the stillness gave us the chance to recover, to rest our eyes from the sky-wide arcs of sensuality that marked the time and place, and our minds from the social excitements, seeing Gregory Peck in the flesh, hearing first-hand descriptions of the brandy-drinking feats of those talented quick-diers, Mark Hellinger and Robert Newton. We followed, in myth, their footsteps as they drained dry the entire cognac supply of Shaftsbury Avenue, as one might walk in the wake of the thirst, torment and death of Dylan Thomas in and around 42nd Street. It was one of my late-night exercises in the padded quietness of our hotel lounge to toss the still rampageous ghosts of these suicidal soaks into the face of the Calvinistic shock I never failed to get from the sight of such a multitude seeking to fill the public eye with an excess of private parts.

Various friends, having me in the very seat of European pleasure, tried to dilute my frown and broaden the curriculum of my delight. One night I was taken along to the Casino and was impressed only by the methods used by the security men to determine our identity, and making sure that we were neither bums nor gangsters. Had they known how much I was going to spend on the tables I would have been thrown on to the foreshore, possibly as a gangster, certainly as a bum. The nature of the games played and the manias of the addicts I could make no sense of. On the way back from the gambling place, I phoned John Knox again and told him that as soon as he wished a return match with the improvident and the lovers of Mary, Queen of Scots, I would try to arrange it.

For some time we were in doubt about the direction our film should take. The younger and heartier members of our team took a simple view of the matter. All they wanted to do was to shoot a thousand reels illustrating from every angle available to the prone and the brave the impact of the sun on near nudity, and apparently wanton willingness. The result, especially if colour spilled over in the meantime from the cinema on to television, would have our viewers in Wales and the West Country of England panting and bubbling during the next winter, their emotions made fluent at the very time of the year when their being would be girdled by frozen water-pipes.

I did not much like the scenario. Sex as a possible competi-

N

tive play in the Olympic Games or the more elastic kind of
Welsh eisteddfod might engage my interest on a screen, but
the juvenile preliminaries of the love act, kissing, ogling,
whistling, peering, I would put down, with after-dinner speak-
ing, as a denial of life, a nerve-twisting nuisance.

We were discussing these themes at a party given at the Carl-
ton by Jack Hylton, Britain's Paul Whiteman of his day and
guiding genius of the television company for which we were
making the film. Someone said that there was an island just off
Cannes on which stood the Château d'If, the fortress from
which Edmond Dantes had escaped in Dumas's *The Count of
Monte Cristo*.

I knew the story well. I had used the chapters describing the
escape as my only French text while teaching a class of mental
vagrants. I had every detail of the incident cut deep in my mind.
The Abbé's beard and fish-bones, Dantes nipping through the
intervening wall like a roach, the substitution of the living body
for the dead, the fifty-pound cannon-balls tied to the sack, the
burial ('the sea is the graveyard of the Château d'If'). A
thousand boys must have left the school with that as their only
phrase of remembered French, and it might, in certain parts of
France, have struck the right conversational chord. A thousand
more, their noses rubbed beyond repair in the Faria-Dantes con-
frontation, left the school with the notion that France must be
an enclosed and gloomy place where the talk was sad, razors
blunt and the means of communication tough.

The people at the party agreed that the Château d'If, thrown
in as a grim antiphony to the lovelies who were keeping the
sand out of sight and the lechers loping, would give us a fine,
dramatic piece. One of our number could see it all, in advance,
vividly: Dantes, seven years in a dungeon, still in his virile
prime, with no other company but a withered abbot, a sound
scholar but nobody's idea of a bride, and an eighteen-foot tun-
nel between them. And just around the corner from the Château
the sunstruck, fame-struck demi-monde. Jack Hylton ordered a
sea-taxi to get us to the Château on the following day.

I looked as pleased and eager as anyone when this idea was

being canvassed. But I knew quite well that we were on the
wrong tack. The Château d'If was off Marseilles, a fair thirty
miles to the east. The only notable prisoner associated with the
Cannes area was the Man in the Iron Mask, who had spent his
adult life in some rocky gaol with his head encased to expiate
his bastardy, treachery, or whatever it was he had done to offend
the ruling dolt. But, having been the one who brought up the
Château d'If in the first place, I said nothing. When the talk is
good and the drinking free, that is not the time for pedantry.
And I learned that rhyme at my mother's knee.

When we boarded the sea-taxi the next day the Château d'If
and Dantes were not mentioned. Everyone it seemed had taken a
decisive peek at the encyclopaedia in between the penultimate
and the last drink. The sea-taxi was fast. It created, at intervals
of ten or so seconds, the equivalent of the sonic boom. Either
that or it was hitting the bottom of the sea. Between these shocks
and the wine-fumes that still hung around the fact of the night
before, I was virtually concussed and opened my eyes only when
invited to take a look at a barred window let into an ochre cliff.
This, I was told, was the cell in which the Man in the Iron Mask
had rusted away in company with his ghastly mask.

We disembarked on the Isle of Lerins. It was about the only
place on this earth where I have broken what one might call
the brochure barrier. It had enchantment and a few million-
aires's yachts all around about. We ate like imperial gluttons
off sea-food and many wines. For the first time I really heard
the bugles of the gastronomes, marked the classic concordances
of substance and liquid, the symmetry of tastes and was then
solemnly unwell in a plantation of palm-trees.

Recovered, I explored the island with Graham Jenkins, who
was with us to cover some film on the festival with commen-
tary in Welsh. Graham is a genial and eloquent young man. He
is a brother of Richard Burton. His basic job is to manage and
expand a new resort called the Afan Lido, which is another
name for Aberavon beach, a curious adjunct of the steel capi-
tal, Port Talbot, a place where dirty air has become a kind of
culture, endlessly discussed and analysed and artfully preserved.

The Afan Lido, as Graham has developed it, is now an enclave of running fun in a stretch of incomparable industrial foulness.

Graham approached Cannes in an aggressive spirit. On several mornings he and I had strolled from the hotel to stare at the small, marcel-waved patch of sand that does duty as a beach. Graham looked at it with scorn. 'Say what you like. It's not a patch on Aberavon. Not a patch.'

He was right. Compared with Cannes, the sands of Aberavon are vast, a secondary Sahara purged at last of a thousand kinds of pollution. Even the local seabirds now caw with less carping inflections.

But even Graham had to concede an insuperable charm to the Isle of Lerins. He listened carefully as I made a very rough translation of a Latin inscription on the arch of the gateway that led to the Benedictine monastery, famous for quietness and home-made liqueurs. 'I shall remember none but the hours that were serene.'

Graham nodded and ran a mildly Jacobinical gaze over the millionaires' yachts and the superbly caparisoned women who lolled on their decks. His eyes can express the same lightnings of blue-green intensity as his brother's; glints of Promethean rage against the ugly imbecilities of all past and present times that have defiled delight and blackened the eyes of what, from the angle of a charitable patience, has been a worthy enough species. I remembered Richard Burton telling me while defining what he called a certain integrity of daftness among the reactionaries of the world: 'It's noteworthy that the enemies of Darwin and the idea of an evolutionary process of an ape as our father, have underlined their point by making monkeys out of men.'

'Serene hours,' said Graham. 'That's what I want for Aberavon, for all our people, for all the old, spoiled places.'

In the harbour at Cannes during our stay was a massive American warship. A press officer of the municipality, thinking we would be interested in all the muscles of Nato, had rattled off for us some of the attributes of this vessel. It was nuclear powered but already so out of date they could expose it without fear to the public eye. Its services gave the men aboard her a cosmos of bland comfort and security. A million doughnuts, with as many cartons of coffee: God knows how many film shows. We told the press officer that his recital made us feel safer about the future of the free world.

Set against the background of that giggling throng of naiads and star-seekers, the ship struck us as an unlovely lump of misdirected skill. Its presence at that particular spot puzzled us. Possibly it was to keep the French awed and the Soviet Union timid. The French didn't seem to look at it; the Soviet Union was nowhere in sight. It made us understand a little better the broad loathing felt for Britain after its period of sticking gunboats in every viable cove on earth. It is without any doubt the most gruesome way of presenting a nation's face to the world.

I asked the cameramen to busy themselves on the homeward trip from the Isle of Lerins, and in honour of the world's taxpayers and the tens of thousands of monks on the island who had dedicated centuries to nothing less sweet than prayer and fine liqueurs, to get some pictures of the battleship. Since it was obsolete they were not likely to be shot by any watchful patriot aboard. Crouched on the most unlikely parts of the sea-taxi, they did so.

Back home in Britain we had a look at the film. It was the anticipated dreary catalogue of near nudes and bijou pornography. Had we shown it as it was one half of the audience would have been asleep, the other half stirred by ancient challenges to go into the street to see what was on offer.

But the shots of the battleship struck a good, deep, sombre note. It gave us an idea for the film's final shape. We inserted into the sequences of sunlight, laughter, vitaminised venery and dreams shots of the teeming dilemmas of our time, incinerated cities, starved children, all the chilling litter left around by the sour-minded monarchs of waste who run our State Departments and Foreign Offices, the men who see war as a logical and palliative extension of their quaking heart valves and corroded kidneys; the whole mess of violence brewed in the pots of our hallowed lunacies.

The film was shown to minute audiences and improved the world not at all. It won a subordinate prize at the Prague Film Festival. Its vague humanitarianism might have made some appeal to the people of those parts. We went up to London to the Czech Embassy to collect the document that would prove we had made a film and won some sort of prize with it. We looked forward to the occasion. We had heard that the East European embassies, for all the sullen mien of so many of their officials, could stage joyous and hard-drinking parties, gushers of vodka and brandies distilled from the world's finest fruit. We must have caught the Czechs on a bad day, some pause in the revels to rededicate themselves to that creative self-discipline which is the protein of the plebs. If we had come along to their Kensington mansion to put down the Embassy dogs we would not have been under firmer control.

There was not a drink in the place, save perhaps the one we might have wrung from the lighter-hearted pamphlets that littered the place. Are there, on this earth, any amiable, welcoming embassies? One of the worst I've run into was the American Consulate at Cardiff when I went in there to sign officially some contract forms for a novel that was to be published in the States. The consul entered slowly, like God, flanked by two aggressive and suspicious minions who addressed me as if they were Mississippi sheriffs opening a Choose Your Chain Gang Week. I went to that consulate again, later, for a visa. The consul was now a lady, as bright and charming as you like. What, as they say, is wrong with the world is that so many public officials project into public circulation so much of the private trouble that bubbles inside them just like the volcanic chaos inside the curious ball we sail along on. All spokesmen of great powers come inevitably to resemble their battleships.

The Czechs gave us our certificate of merit. Speeches were made deploring the men and politics that kept Europe looking and sounding like a corral of imbecilic cows. There were reporters present. I do not think the event justified their presence. They had probably been lured by that banner with the magnetic device: free drink. One of them got me in a corner. He wanted to know if I thought that the award might make me politically suspect. The atmosphere at the time was more than usually spy-crazy, and he might have thought that I had patterned the nudes in my film in such a way as to betray to the East every tittle of our secret sewage-farm defences west of the Cotswolds.

To ease the great sense of responsibility brought on by these thoughts I rested my arm on a china cupboard that had been re-varnished that very day. It was strong varnish. After fifteen minutes of leaning immobility it took the reporter and a junior Embassy attaché to tear me loose.

I still have the stain of it on my sleeve. I will keep it there. On the few occasions when I go out to pronounce on inter-national affairs, I flash it into view to prove my living link with the subject. My only tangible credential, a stiff sleeve, pointing nowhere.

*

We had planned a journey to Spain. Its point was to make a film that would show glimpses of Holy Week and of the cities the Moors had left behind in the slow anguish of their de-parture.

The journey began with a jolt or two. One of our com-panions capped his last evening in London with a dose of fish-poisoning. On our way to the airport there was some muttering doubt as to whether he would be able to make it. He did. While the plane was still over the Pyrenees he wanted to leave it the short way. I told him that those mountains were bad to land on. He stuck it out, keeping us on edge and wearing out a hostess. I was not upset. It is nice to enter a country as sad as Spain with a bit of abrasive suffering at one's side.

When we landed at Madrid the place was blotted out by a cloud-burst. For this I was not ungrateful. In any medium a little obliquity and a few veils help. A freak gale almost over-turned the taxi that took us into the city, and whipped the meter into an increase of five shillings.

We stayed at the Hotel Fenix, named after Lope de Vega,

known as the Phoenix or the Monster of Nature, a portent, the Frank Sinatra of his age. He wrote two thousand plays and had as many mistresses and died in Holy Orders, which no phoenix ever did.

The first thing we got at the hotel was a message from our cameramen, who were bringing the equipment overland in their own transport. The Spaniards at the frontier had saluted Eurovision and their hopes of integration into Europe by impounding the cameras and slapping a bitter impost on them. We were shocked. We had thought the Spanish Embassy in London had given us a clear permission to penetrate Spain and film anything we fancied of a cultural sort.

We went to an agent to see if this fix could be loosened. I spoke to him. It would be impossible to expedite the release of the cameras. Pre-Easter traffic was intense, the officials at full stretch. The room in which we spoke was high-vaulted.

'Impossible?' I would say.

'*Francamente imposible*,' he said. We said it together.

'*Francamente imposible*.' Both our voices were low and anxious and brought down plenty of echo from the tall ceiling. The whole ambience became intolerably operatic. Convinced that the agent was expecting us to cough up with a fee as large as the impost, we left.

We began to frequent the British Embassy. We drank ale at low prices in the Embassy Club. It was a small bar with a dartboard. The diplomats and their helpers regarded us with that unique disdain that bureaucrats have for interlopers. The conversation was both discontinuous and shallow. One was relieved to be struck now and then by a dart. One welcomed a visible wound.

On our first evening there, in a lull in some talk about dagoes, I heard a ghostly, low-pitched yawping. At first I thought it was some Foreign Office talent putting our case for Gibraltar in a coarser tone than usual. Someone pointed out of the window. A vast, dark peahen was draped over the wall of the courtyard, shrieking its heart out. It might have been lamenting, on the Embassy's behalf, Britain's lost empire and travelling confi-

dence. It was doing no such thing. It was pleading for the re-
turn of her peacock which had been kidnapped or eaten by a
local group who often circled the Embassy's walls on missions
of ill-will.

We went to see one of the directors of Spain's Film and TV
Centre. He was an intense, whispering man. We tried to per-
suade him to help us get our apparatus off the excisemen's
hook. He made no direct reply. He spoke of an international
conference he had attended on the documentary cinema. His
mind was fixed on a worship of Robert Flaherty. He kept say-
ing, 'Ah, si, *Louisiana Story*,' and he gave an imitation of alliga-
tors patrolling a bayou to show that for him a thing once seen
was not forgotten. He didn't help us at all.

Our first trip out of the city was to Segovia. My first
experience of motor traffic in Spain had burned my nerve-ends.
I put out the smoulder in a bar in the middle of the town. The
only other person in the bar was a half-drunk, wholly demented
shoe-black. He kept banging the lid of his professional box to
the rhythm of some inward story of torment. I did not want
my shoes cleaned. I said so. He dropped his box on my feet. It
was heavier than I had imagined.

He took my mind off the Roman aqueduct outside, straddling
the town in ugly majesty, as dull and durable as the echoes of
the brass-headed Emperor Charles, who hung a lot of weavers
here in 1521 and coffined normal democratic impulses in Spain
for three hundred years.

Our next outing was jollier. We were told that in a place
called Cuenca the Easter action was high, a turn-out of the de-
vout that would galvanise even the most torpidly antipathetic
outsider. The approach to Cuenca is a long fierce downward
slope. We saw notices all conveying the same message. '*Aten-
cion a los frenos.*'

'What does that mean?'

The hinges of my vocabulary had worked loose over the
years. 'Watch the ash-trees,' I said.

My friends were puzzled but they were stuck with me as an
interpreter. We all admired the trees on the densely afforested

hills. They did not look like ash-trees, but we felt we had to respect the men who had put up those notices. Then smoke started to rise from the front of the car. The crisis tightened the hinges of my vocabulary. The notices had said, 'Watch the brakes.' After this first moment of translation under stress my reputation as an interpreter was dark and the brake linings ashen. I gave a promise never to translate anything again in a context of trees.

When we got to Cuenca the town was coming to the boil. We could hear the first drumbeats from the tiny square in which the procession was being marshalled. The sidewalks were thronged by a great number of deprived and unstable people, most of them seated. They would normally, in a place as chronically ashamed as Spain, have been hidden away. But this was the day of revelation, exposure. They were smiling, intense, waving, shouting. Their frenzy added an inch to the air of impending miracles.

The procession, for one brought up on the meagre rituals of chapeldom, induces a potent sense of alienation. The Stations of the Cross are heavy, detailed and borne on poles by hooded penitents, many of whom do not look up to it. One of the bearers seemed incredibly old and frail. He was swaying under the burden a good foot more either way than his colleagues, and he was clearly regarded as a nuisance to the order of march. He wore spectacles under his full, conical hat. His eyes were bulging. A sudden shaft of sunlight into the shadowed street blinded him and set his feet shuffling. A butterfly flying within an inch of his eye-slit finished him off. He lurched into the crowd. He was helped back to his post by a Civil Guard. Somebody suggested that he was too tired to go on. He screamed a denial and I heard someone mutter that he was the only man in Cuenca who proved his piety by three strokes yearly.

A very old woman stood on a balcony awaiting the arrival of the first great Christ-figure. Her face was dark, a web of suggestions built around one central wrinkle. It suggested a life through which the whole demented Spanish past had moved with incinerating fury. The head of the first Christ-figure came

up to her shoulder. She smiled as she touched its face and said,
'How are you, Jesus?' for all the world as if Christ were a cosy
familiar who knocked on her door and called in for a chat
several times a day.

A girl of about nine, walking alone, wore a silver-paper
crown and a robe of white sequined gauze, carried a lighted
candle, a tiny simulation of the Virgin Mary. She was aware in
full of her own beauty. Her face was as still as the candle's
flame in the morning's windless air. A lad in the crowd, an
urchin of about her own age, shouted some ribald irreverence
at her. She did not smile. She left the procession and walked up
to him. She put the arm that bore the candle around his
shoulders in a gesture that was a distillation of all patience and
compassion, then, with her candle, gave his right elbow a
thorough roasting.

The boy gave out a savage cry but his neighbours slapped
him back when he tried to chase the lovely and ruthless cherub.
The middle one of three ponderous political bosses following
immediately behind a military band reacted badly. He had been
disquieted already by having his ear sandwiched between layers
of blasting brass. The yelp of the singed boy sent him over the
edge. He went greener than his exquisite olive uniform.

Granada was one of our larger targets. The traffic movements
of this place are tortuous. It is almost as tough getting into the
city now as it was for the Christian Knights who plundered
their way into its citadel in 1492 when Columbus sailed the
ocean blue, and Granada slipped from the hands of Boabdil,
the last Moorish king.

I was sitting in the gardens of the Alhambra. The palace is
a fretted brothel in russet stone and none the worse for that. I
was brooding on the sinister fruits for the European mind of
the Christian triumph in Spain, and pondering the plight of
those who get the business from the brooms of time and
violence.

I heard my name called. I thought at first it was Boabdil the
refugee. I have, in my time, achieved some striking bits of
rapport with fragments of the past. Once when writing a novel

on the Chartists I got so involved in that ragged old shindig I almost collected a five-year stretch for unlawful assembly.

It was not Boabdil. It was a woman, sticking her head from behind a carob-tree and calling me. She came into view followed by two other ladies. The first one said, 'We are a busload of women from Penrhiwceiber, near Pontypridd. We are staying at Torremolinos. We know your cousin, Merlin Thomas. He's got a ladies' choir. He's lovely.'

My Moorish thoughts, with Boabdil and his vanished night-ingales, limped into silence. I walked with the women down to the town. We had tea and a tremendous chat about Penrhiwceiber.

From Granada we next went west to the Atlantic. To Cadiz where there is a street called the Avenue of Hamilcar Barca, father of Hannibal, and a beach with a load of litter that looks as if it might have been started by Hamilcar. Then Seville, where Holy Week has a pagan gloss. Elegant horsemen lying almost flat on their horses' backs in their effort to look His-panically proud and erect. Women with so many flowers in their hair they move in a double-yoke of dandruff and hay-fever. And the people giving an acclaim to Mrs Jacqueline Kennedy that would have done justice to an empress in the noon of her dominion.

Then back to Madrid where I lost my luggage.

Unencumbered, I decided to walk home.

*

For me, from childhood, the name and fact of Russia have been loud on the wind. In my valley the militants peered into every corner, looking for powers to subvert, pieties to thrash, blacklegs to harass, bailiffs to outrage, orthodoxy to knock, and usually finding them. Occasionally these subversive lads would be collared and whipped off to gaol. We took an operatic joy in their martyrdom.

In packed public meetings we groaned with sympathy when-ever an orator pointed his tongue at the judge who had put them inside and the turnkeys who kept them there. When they were released we awaited their homecoming on the town square. They would be significantly wan, a stone or so thinner after a few months of being off chips, good cheer and salutary agitation. We applauded them until hoarseness or the pitch dark intervened.

The victims had their reward. As true bullfighters of the dialectic they touched some nerve of sexual excitement and, like any Spanish torero, seemed to wear a tail of compliant girls. A more lavish accolade was a trip to Russia.

I have an impression of a whole stream of these lads trudging down the hill, bearing old and fissile suitcases, on the first lap of a journey to Moscow, for ideological stiffening, or to the Crimea for an infusion of socialised sun and fun. It always surprised me to think that Yalta might coax a smile out of these frowning paladins, for they were an earnest crew.

When they returned they spoke copiously of the rough, muscled paradise coming swiftly to birth on the other side of the Baltic. One, I recall, brought back a fine line in sad, Ukrainian folk-songs, which he sang in the chip-shop. It disgusted the chip-merchant, a man marbled in ancient loyalties who was waiting for the first Marquis of Bute to stop dallying in stupid death and come back to oust the local socialist M.P. The rest of us, sensitive to sad songs, broad vowels and plangent sounds from distant places, shed exciting tears over our shared length of hake.

For the conformist and timid, this trickle of heretics into the Soviet Union took on the qualities of a sinister folk-tale, as if Russia were an unbreached medieval forest into which fair children were abducted and slain. If anyone were not seen around for several weeks, no one ever thought he might be a fugitive from debt or boredom. He was in Minsk or Kirovabad, wearing a commissar's badge, stroking tractors, blaspheming and getting the Celt a bad name around Whitehall.

In my early twenties, savouring a post-graduate gloom in an emphatically pre-graduate world, I stood in a darkened convenience on Porth Square. Some splenetic ratepayer had stoned

o

the light-bulbs to discourage further investment in this kind of amenity. Two men came in. One of them was talking. Even outside that sounding crypt his voice would have been strikingly loud and dramatic.

I heard my name mentioned. 'Do you know who he is?' The second man muttered that he did not know, did not care. He was in trouble with the shadows, groping his way towards his niche and occasionally going headlong over patches of loose floor material. The vandals had won a prize with that convenience.

The first man went on. 'A scholar, a book reader. Gaunt bloke. Very stooped. Wild eyes. Wrote a pamphlet denouncing decency, tithes and the Minister of Labour, Mr Ernest Brown, a man of God and a voice of thunder in the right shaped pulpit. A chronic denouncer, this Thomas. Do you know where he is now?'

The second man's hand had now landed with stunning force against the wall above his niche and he was caring even less.

'He's in Moscow,' said the first man, 'being trained as a spy. So if you see him, when and if he comes back, don't go blurting out any secrets. Even if it's only about our Sunday School hiring a marquee at Barry this year for the tea. God knows what the Russians might make of that. All those Christians under one canvas roof. Happy, relaxed, replete, vulnerable. Keep it to yourself if that Thomas is about. Let him hear it and he'll be spying full pelt. He'll rig up his little wireless and that Stalin will be in the know by Thursday.'

The second man, more confident now about the dark, said he would be vigilant. They shuffled out of the convenience. When I had recovered from the shock of discovering that I might be trained for anything, I followed them.

It was not until an epoch later that I clapped eyes on the Kremlin. By this time the name and fact of Russia had become less emotive, sang more quietly on the wind. The old hot ardours had cooled and greyed into clinker. The world had been savaged, concussed and had become quieter. The warriors of the Marxist word had slipped into apathy or the earth. Their voices were not heard save in some bit of sardonic late-night musing.

My own rancours had shrunk to an obsessional loathing of social columns and a manic brooding on how and why Morton's modest little Elizabethan Fork had become the multilateral fiscal scythe I had spent my life failing to dodge.

One echo remained. He was a man called Ike, a long-distance dissident, and during the whole period of our being neighbours, ailing on a broad front. He was one of the people who had been dispatched to the Soviet Union in the early thirties for a bout of curative calm after having been in gaol for resisting evictions.

Ike and his brother also carried a small, illegal printing press about the town in a clothes basket, and on this press he would print notices about the date of the imminent rising of the breechless against the over-clothed. The few notices to roll from this press, a pre-Caxton job by all reports, were so dim and illegible it was thought likely that Ike's brochure of instructions had left out all reference to ink.

People who stepped briskly from the Bolshevik camp to the spiritualist (a curiously large number) tried in later years to contact Ike's posthumous self to ask him, out of simple curiosity, what date he had had in mind.

I got to know Ike well in his last years. Illness and penury had made a shabby cartoon of the lad he had been at the start of the journey. He sat woodenly on the knee of the petrifying past and muttered with ventriloquial sadness. He was being tormented by the flagging momentum of his blood and dreams. He was also being bullied out of life by his wife, a fractious, abusive and powerful woman, a sergeant-major of dour convention.

Occasionally Ike would point out to me the house in Penygraig where Trotsky, then a fleeting messenger of the Comintern, getting the Rhondda into marching order for the last advance on what Ike called 'the Pyramids of the last Pharaohs', had stayed and eaten chips out of paper.

He never seemed to point to the same house twice and it was

clear that his memories were failing in point and coherence. It turned out that the man who had stayed in Penygraig was not Trotsky at all but a person called Kautsky, an itinerant German jeweller, neat in his habits, non-political and averse to chips.

Ike also sang a Russian song. It was Ukrainian. He claimed to have learned it in a village where, briefly, he had known some beaker of special enchantment. The melody was vague. Every time he sang it his wife, in a voice of amplified thunder, she told him to shut up. One sultry afternoon Ike did so, for good.

I was reminded of Ike on my first journey to the Soviet Union. I flew there in an Ilyushin jet. I expected the customary swift flow of drink that alone makes these experiences credible. In the first hour I got one boiled sweet. I doubted whether I could continue to live at this pace for the next two and a half hours. But at the first hour's end came food. My cutlery slid at once to the floor from my sloping table. I could do nothing about it. I never undo my seat belt once I have secured it. One day I will carry this phobia to a point where I will arrive at the hotel of my destination city dragging the plane behind me.

During the third hour vodka flowed like the Don but less quietly. My neighbour was a man who had left Russia as a boy and was returning after thirty-six years. He was eager to see a village in south-west Russia whose name he could not at that moment recall. Some loving uncle had lived there. We kept pace in our drinking, bottle for bottle, laughing at the price every time we took a sip, like children at a newly discovered sea.

He began to cry. I began to sing to him the song Ike had sung. Coming from me it sounded even vaguer than it had at the start. I asked him if he knew it. He could not place it. But it served to remind him, in some mysterious way, of the name of the village he wished to revisit.

And that, on an earth where the lost are a nation in themselves, is something.

*

My links with America are tenuous. My grandfather emigrated there in the 1880s and my father was born there. While seeking work and a home in Ohio they ran into a volley of shots from a posse of Pinkerton strike-breakers, and wheeled into another posse from the strikers who were just beginning to get Pinkerton's length.

My grandfather was a carpenter in love with tranquillity and beat it back to his joiner's shed in Glamorgan at a speed that had the officials in Ellis Island, unused to any kind of eastern flow, doing double-takes well into the new century.

The effect of this experience on my father was not great. He claimed to have learned some songs of the Civil War from the lips of veterans. He sang these songs very quietly and the tone was further muffled by having never less than four or five sceptical sons grouped around him to make out the meaning and urge him to sing up. But he said the memory of those veterans was still so potent it crushed his voice beneath a load of emotion. He was not much of a singer and we took his word for it.

He also showed me once a pair of tiny, red, shrivelled slippers. These, he said, were what he wore as a child on the liner in which he did his homeward trip. On a day of good light and high curiosity I examined these slippers with care. On them I saw the name of a noted shoe-shop in the lower Rhondda and, working out my father's putative age when he came back, he would have needed to break all the bones in both feet to get the slippers on, on or off a liner.

But the sight of those corrugated relics filled him with such luminous pathos we did not press the issue. He seemed to suggest that my grandfather had been a poltroon, that he had taken flight, beaten his way back to penury when his hands were virtually already on the very knobs of the golden doors to Rockefeller's throne room.

My father would end this recital by cursing the cowardice that haunts most male members of his tribe, traceable, he said, to the all-white loaf, a wantonly diffused compassion and the winter of 1909, when four branches of the family lost their roofs and their confidence.

That rattle of gun-fire, he never ceased to claim, between the Pinkertons and their enemies just south of Newtown, Ohio, could have been the call to glory for all our clan. But he never really looked as if he believed it. Nor did we.

So, on my first visit to the States, there was no surge of spiritual overtones, no sense of returning to a birthright narrowly missed and poignantly regretted. The whole experience, despite its underlying clamour, was full of abrupt, unsettling silences.

On the outward plane my neighbour was a Nebraskan reformer, against sex and for after-shave lotion. He was pious and clean to a point that made both these harmless qualities seem sinister. He was a spokesman for some branch of the Moral Rearmament movement and he never failed to speak.

He told me how very lucky we were to be moving away from the pitch-black flippancy and corruption of continental Europe. He said that Britain could not afford to be complacent. He added that even Cardiff, while not yet as blatant as Rotterdam, could, with profit to the pious, be watched and laved.

As we edged into the last hour of the flight, he started peering out of the window. I thought he was taking this chance of checking on the state of sin in New York while the sinners could not see him. I was on the point of asking him what he had spotted in Cardiff that I had missed when he said that he wanted to show me something remarkable about our first view of America's east coast. It had something to do with currents, hot and cold. He was phobic about them. He was in as fierce disagreement with Humboldt as he was with H. L. Mencken.

He shouted in my ear that the phenomenon would be within view inside two minutes, and when he had finished with this detail he was going to slip me a few facts about Cardiff that would put me solidly behind his own cleansing ethic and rippling banner. He jabbed his finger at the smudge of land and water below. He began to announce the theory that was to make a patsy out of Humboldt.

I did not hear a word. A mammoth fall of wax cut off my ears as the plane lurched into a long convulsion. I was told later that I should have been given boiled sweets to counteract this condition, but I had been overlooked when the bag went around, probably in the belief that a head bearing as nay-saying an expression as mine was, in an American context, better off deaf. Anyway, deaf I was.

I tried lip-reading, because I have always wished to know more about currents of water and sin. But the man's ardour was doing things to his mouth and could have yielded nothing but a twisted message. I gave up. I sat still and tried to forget the terrifying marble stillness in my head, hoping it would not turn out to be an omen and knowing that it would.

I stayed at one of the mellowest hotels in New York, as mossy with ancient ways and graces, by New York standards, as a Cotswold village. From the first day the city took bites out of my nerves that made me tetchy as a hunted wolf.

For the first morning I used the bar of the New Weston as a cocoon from inside which to nibble slowly towards contact with the sounds, feel and murderous moves of Peter Stuyvesant's engrossed and bewildering burg. An odd thing happened. I have a habit of holding a drink in my hand for long periods. The amount of ice in the glass and the destructive proportion of gin poured in with the tonic landed me with two cases of frostbite to every one of delirium.

During that first session I was engaged in talk with an executive of a chemical firm from California. He showed me photographs of his plastics products and his children in that order. He was very drunk. He explained that he had just flown in and the time-difference had added a full bottle of bourbon to his normal intake. He showed me a plastic skull-cap he had patented which increased the catchment range of the aural cavities and created such a hullaballoo around the mind it took one's thoughts off thirst.

I did not try to work that out. I explained that I had to be getting along to prepare my first impression of the city. He said the most vital impression of America was to be seen shortly in that bar. It was the world series on television.

He took me to a table to watch it. He explained the game to me. His commentary was passionate, loud and meaningless. He noted and footnoted the fine points of every blow and canter in the contest. They had turned out the lights in our corner to give us a better view of the screen. My eyes kept colliding with the swizzle-stick which, in the gloom, I had forgotten to take from the glass. Stupefaction and blindness lumbered along in a competition of their own.

The Californian's account of how the Dodgers were facing up to their current crisis was now getting mixed up with the story of how he had routed some business rival a year before. He showed me the photographs again. I got them mixed up and I told him one of the plastics products was the spit image of him.

My incomprehension rushed into a high, fruitless summer. Things were not helped by the fact that the television screen was now receiving, under the splitting impact of the Manhattan towers all around, four pictures from different stations. Even the Californian was having difficulty in isolating the baseballers from the other intruding images, among which there seemed to be a high incidence of gnomes and rabbits, introduced by men looking like Jimmy Savile and sounding like Lord Hill, a disquieting tug on the senses.

Then there was silence. The head of my companion was no longer alongside mine. He had slumped forward and had landed courteously and quietly on the table. There were no longer any pictures on the television screen. Some clients, who hated whichever side was winning in the match we had been watching and who had been driven into a kind of delirium by the darkness and general hush of the bar, had switched the set off. Feeling that these things added up pretty plainly to the end of an experience, I edged out.

Once more, before I left that patch of teeming loudness, I was to know another sudden withdrawal of sound. The day before my return I did a private tour by taxi. I had come, with the passing of a fortnight, to find the barking truculence of the New York taxi-drivers less frightening. I could now get into a cab without staring at the driver's portrait stuck up on the dashboard and wondering if I was going to be abducted or just chauffeured. They are the most clamant bacilli of a body with whose life all is not well.

My last driver was a typical member of the guild. He was a tough and garrulous joker. He ran through the whole spectrum of social and political phenomena in and out of America, and had not a good word to say about any of them. From Roosevelt clear across to Gandhi; bums, jerks, hustlers. The only good thing about the United Nations was that its headquarters were near enough to the East River to permit, one wise, quiet morning, the ducking and drowning of the delegates.

Not to be outdone in confused thinking, I started to sing that hymn 'Thy Kingdom Come, On Bended Knee', which speaks up plainly for sanity, hope and peace. This hymn, I explained, was given in every British hymnal the code name 'Moscow'. The driver asked me to repeat. I did so. I could hear the breeze of unknowing stiffen across the Hudson. He paused to listen for a perplexed second and turned his head as if mentally measuring the distance to the nearest bend of the East River.

'Singing, eh?' he said. 'Well, dere's no amusement tax on dat, I reckon.' We both laughed but without warmth.

He took me through Central Park as dusk was falling. I had been fed with legends about this vast playground. How, from behind every shadow and bush, came nightly delegations of rapists, muggers, the blank-faced, hurting envoys of the moon, the twitching, killing ambassadors of the world's greatest act of urban madness. Was this so? I asked the driver. Did this seemingly tranquil place become at night the human equivalent of a convention of piranha fish?

The driver was now on firmer territory. He had read about piranha fish in a *Digest* and had once been mugged. He stopped the car and ran a window down. 'Listen,' he said. I listened. The night was full of sounds. I tried to sort them out. Feet among grass, crickets giving out messages, squirrels at their nuts, birds coping with the dark. I suggested this list to the driver. He shook his head.

'Not a bird or bat or cricket among dem. Dey are de savages all around, all moving. I don't know where dey come from. But dey are savages. . . .' He switched back with a grunt that shook the car. 'Taxes. Taxes. I eat Taxes. I drink Taxes. But no tax on savagery.' He turned round to face me fully. I have never seen a man so totally like his own passport photograph.

'My name is Maroulis. My father was a Greek person. Came from a deadbeat village that died because there was never enough water. I never saw it. But let me tell you some of the . . .' He peered at me. I was pondering the matchless idiocy of all human aggregations of more than three thousand and my face was darkening under the weight and taste of the thought. I was looking too pensive for Maroulis.

The silence had become physically distasteful. He ran the window up and started a ride of crazy speed back to the hotel. He took my fare without a word and did not even return my good night.

The next day I stood at Kennedy Airport and nodded at the fugitive, eastward-homing ghost of my grandfather.

*

The mind, the body move in shrinking circles. My being has never edged more than a few inscrutable inches from the kitchen of the house where I lived as a boy, a teeming and tempestuous place, cocoon of myths and spinning absurdities. From its seemingly always open door we had a mountain in full view. It was called Arthur's Crown. Once, long ago, we had a sad and noble king called Arthur. This mountain had a sad and noble shape. So we called it Arthur's Crown. It was very beautiful. It was bare except for a fringe of stunted trees across its top, bent and crouched by the winds that blew in from the sea.

I felt sorry for those trees and I was relieved when I climbed the slope for the first time, touched them and found them stronger and happier-looking than they had ever looked from the valley-bed. That mountain became the centre of my heart and imagination. My father often pointed to it. He said that one day he would take us over it.

Beyond the mountain, with its magical velvet paths moving through the high summer ferns, in another valley, there was a town called Mountain Ash. There, said my father, we had a lot of aunts and cousins.

'They are beautiful,' he said, 'those aunts and cousins. As beautiful as that mountain. But shorter, you understand. And they are kind. They have a big house. Tall windows and flowers in them all. They will be waiting for us. They will see us coming down the hillside. They will come out to meet us. They have money. They will give you money.'

That last sentence clinched it. Things were tough. We were even borrowing from the mice. And they were appealing for protection to the International Bank.

A Sunday morning came when my father took us for the first time on the long hill-top walk to Mountan Ash. The path to the mountain-top was steep and treacherous underfoot. My father walked fast. To our small untrained legs the mountain seemed like a wall and we seemed like flies. Short of clutching my father's jacket and boarding him like a bus we could never have kept up. Fortunately my father knew everyone who passed and talked with them, discussing their problems without being able to do much to solve them.

As we approached the top we were full of a sense of an enchantment about to be revealed, touched, tasted. Enchanted it was. That sea of ferns, endless to the eye of a child. A world of kind and golden light. Larks singing with a force that made it seem they were trying to burst their way into one of the local choirs. And we would sing back at them. Larks and sheep looking so gentle and intelligent one spoke to them and got answers of a kind.

It was and is the land of my emotions. To the north stretch the ranges of mountains that make Wales a land of mysterious and exclusive valleys; to the south the channel that divides us from England, full, as dusk fell, of the winking, tempting lights of ships going to or coming from the great waters of the West.

A dozen times we started on that Sunday walk with my father. But we never got to Mountain Ash. We never got to see those aunts and cousins whose goodness and beauty would have brought new dimensions of joy into our lives.

Halfway across the plateau there is a village called Llan-wonno. In the village is a pub called The Tavern of the Fountain. Near the pub was a spring and its water was sweet. This made no appeal to my father. He always considered water-drinking an inferior experience. By the time he got to the village he had developed a thirst it would have taken two fire-brigades to put out. He knew the landlord and landlady of the pub.

Although the pub was officially closed on Sunday my father was always welcomed in, and for three or four hours in the cool, stone-flagged bar he would sip beer and talk to his friends about the people they had known who now rested in the grave-yard just over the road from the pub.

'I can't think of a healthier place to be buried,' my father would say. 'No noise, no smoke, no traffic. A treat.'

As my father drank and chatted the afternoon away, the talk grew less solemn with the passing of every pint, and we heard the gales of laughter come rocking through the pub's closed door. We stayed outside, drinking lemonade and watching the wind make a kind of visual music among the ferns. If it were a day of great heat we would go to the shadowy banks of an ice-cold stream nearby. We would fish and catch nothing. Or we would bathe and catch colds. But even sneezing we never lost the sense of being in an unsmirched paradise.

We never managed to complete the journey to the neigh-bouring valley, to the big house where the group of fair and benevolent women and maidens would be watching for us in their flowered windows, to accord us a warm and silver wel-come. After a session in the pub my father would be too weary even to start the second leg of his journey.

Using my brother and myself as two short crutches he would make his uneven way back to our house. There he would sit by the kitchen window, staring at the lovely mountain, a look of sad remorse on his face, vowing that one day, like a latter-day Moses, he would lead us all the way to that promised land in Mountain Ash where the cousins and aunts would be waiting to usher us into a heaven of affection, a blinding shower of tarts, toffees and threepenny bits. He never did.

I was at the Fountain Inn one evening last summer. Our intention was to cross the plateau all the way to Mountain Ash and fix once and for all the location of that shrine of loveliness that had slipped furtively in and out of my father's talk and dreams so many years ago.

The whole day had been a throne of sweet sensations. The walk over the mountain-top had been exquisite, the air and the grass a matching velvet. We had meat and wine in the dining-room. We were in a fine, rare mood of abdication. We talked of the futility of power and spoke with relish of Edward II who had been betrayed, captured in a dingle nearby and trundled to some English fortress, there to be abominably executed. So we were told by our teacher in the Primary School whose authority was total, and who had compiled a bulging dossier on local treacheries.

Then the inn filled up with a rush. It was a visit by the whole of the Pendyrus Male Voice Choir, singers of matchless passion from the Little Rhondda. There was pause for a drink of welcome and the pianist struck a rich chord for silence. A quartet of ancients were discussing parliamentary government with such gall the fabric of Westminster must have winced. Alongside them two men were trying to recall the year in which a brilliant black sheep called Caradoc had outsmarted a whole panel of sheep-dogs. It took three more rich chords to make these debators fall still.

The choir roared into a piece about the irrelevance of death and the certain prospect of renewal. They then eased the strain and brought all our doubts back with a very negative item called 'Ten Green Bottles'. Then, the midsummer dusk outstanding, they sang one of the loveliest of the quiet carols. The night put on a cap of gold. I was home, at my earth's warm centre. The scared monkey was back in the branches of his best-loved tree. I've never had any truly passionate wish to be elsewhere.